Chicago Tribune

Crossroads, USA

Discovering American Culture and Language with the Daily Newspaper

Robert Hughes

National Textbook Company
a division of NTC/CONTEMPORARY PUBLISHING COMPANY
Lincolnwood, Illinois USA

Editorial Director: Cindy Krejcsi

Executive Editor: Mary Jane Maples

Editor: Michael O'Neill

Design Manager: Ophelia M. Chambliss

Cover Design: Annette Spadoni

Interior Design: Design Associates

Cover Illustration: Tony Stone Images

Production Manager: Margo Goia

ISBN: 0-8442-0455-2

Published by National Textbook Company,

a division of NTC/Contemporary Publishing Company,

4255 West Touhy Avenue,

Lincolnwood (Chicago), Illinois 60646-1975 U.S.A.

© 1998 NTC/Contemporary Publishing Company

890 VL 0987654321

Contents

Introduction

Crossroads, USA is a reading skills text built around recently published articles from the *Chicago Tribune*. These articles have been selected for the light they shine on people in the United States: how they live, what they think, and why they behave the way they do.

One of the most prominent and respected newspapers in the United States, the *Chicago Tribune* is a wonderful source for information about American culture. Since 1847 the *Tribune* has chronicled the growth of Chicago from a booming frontier town to the major world city it is today. Chicago has always been a sort of crossroads for newcomers seeking a new life in the United States. Today, with over a hundred ethnic groups populating its diverse neighborhoods, Chicago mirrors the dynamically changing culture of the United States.

The articles in *Crossroads, USA* reflect the life of this very American city. They reveal aspects of the world of business and work, U.S. lifestyles, views of the nation and community, the role of sports, leisure time, religion, food, and home life. Here you will read about the changing Chicago community of Pilsen, a neighborhood where a number of historic events have occurred; a teacher of English as a second language who has published a book of his students' stories about coming to the United States; the excitement in Green Bay, Wisconsin, when the town's football team, the Green Bay Packers, won the Super Bowl for the first time in many years; a church that wants its members to have fun; an unusual construction company that builds "healthy houses"; and many more.

These articles will help you improve your reading skills while you learn about life in the United States. The exercises that accompany each selection will help you understand the articles' main points, vocabulary, and idioms and help spark lively discussion. In addition, the reading strategies you learn can be applied in almost any other reading you do, from magazines and novels to business reports and textbooks.

Additional attention is given to improving newspaper skills in the text's ten "Focus on Culture" sections. The first Focus section gives an overview of the newspaper and introduces the ways in which newspapers reveal culture. The other nine sections, placed at the end of each section of the text, deal with specific aspects of culture as revealed in newspaper stories.

These Focus sections describe the kinds of information you can expect to find in the newspaper and give practice in recognizing and analyzing different types of articles.

The material accompanying each reading selection is organized as follows:

Previewing the Article

- introduces the topic of the article and provides background information helpful in understanding the article
- provides discussion questions to stimulate interest in the article and to activate prior knowledge about the topic
- suggests specific information to look for as you read

Getting the Message

- focuses on key points of the article by using exercise types such as true/false and multiple choice
- offers an opportunity to confirm your understanding of the article by comparing your answers with the Comprehension Check at the back of the book

Expanding Your Vocabulary

- provides practice in determining the meanings of words and phrases through context
- groups related words (about occupations, money, geographical features, etc.) to aid in comprehension and retention of vocabulary
- encourages analysis of both denotations and connotations of words
- helps to distinguish between homonyms and other easily confused words
- provides practice in building vocabulary by understanding word parts

Working with Idioms and Expressions

- defines key idioms and expressions from the article
- provides practice in using idioms and expressions in context

Analysis of Key Features

Each section includes exercises titled "Making Sense of Sentences," "Analyzing Paragraphs," or "Focusing on Style and Tone." These exercises examine more sophisticated elements of the article, such as

- sentences that include contrasting ideas, conditional clauses, participles used as adjectives, appositives, and other elements of complex and compound sentences
- inferences, figures of speech, and ironic and paradoxical statements
- paragraph development and the ways in which various paragraphs relate to each other and to the main point of the article
- elements of style, such as the nonfiction writer's use of storytelling techniques

Talking and Writing

- Suggests several topics relating to issues in the article for oral and/or written discussion
- Encourages thinking beyond the article to the implications and long-term significance of its message

We hope you enjoy the articles in *Crossroads, USA* and the accompanying exercises and activities. We also hope this text will inspire you to spend some time each day reading a newspaper and discovering the culture of the United States through its pages.

Focus on Culture

How to Read the Newspaper for Information About Culture

Reading a daily newspaper is an excellent way to find out about culture—the values, attitudes, customs, and overall way of life of the people. How do people live in the United States? What do they think is important? How does their political system work? What do they think is funny? What do they think is news? The newspaper provides answers to these kinds of questions daily.

In this Focus section, you will learn about some general features of newspapers that can aid you in learning about U.S. culture on your own.

Headlines and Culture

Because headlines are written to attract the reader to the story, they are a good indication of what readers find important. But because they are short, clever, and often use words with double meanings, headlines can be somewhat difficult to understand fully. But even the more hard-to-read headlines usually give a good hint of an article's main subject matter. Note the following types of headlines:

- **Sentence headlines.** Many headlines, while making a direct statement about the subject of the article, also play with words to attract readers. For example, a sentence headline for a story in the *Chicago Tribune* about the weather reads "Cold snaps shut last week's warmth." The verb *snaps,* indicating a quick closing of a door or of jaws, also plays with another term, *cold snap,* a sudden, brief period of cold weather. Another headline about a peaceful Christmas demonstration in Yugoslavia reads "Serbs fire kisses at the police." The verb *fires* hints at the fact that the demonstrators aren't firing or shooting guns.
- **Phrase headlines.** Other headlines are phrases that imply a shortened sentence. One story from the *Tribune* about Russian President Boris Yeltsin says, "Russian leader back in hospital." Here merely the verb *to be* is left out after *leader.* Sometimes, headlines consist of a noun and phrase, such as "Era of Discontent" for an article about parents' dissatisfaction with television. Some headlines are phrases made more active by using forms of verbs. For example, "Tooning up kids" is the headline for an article about how commercials shown in movie theaters affect children. This headline uses a play on words, or *pun.* The children see cartoons and the term "tune up" means to make a car engine run smoothly. Here "tooning up" means persuading the children to buy certain products.
- **Headlines requiring background knowledge.** Probably the most difficult headlines to understand are those requiring previous knowledge of names, places, organizations, or popular culture. One article in the *Tribune* is entitled "Last tango in the high school gymnasium." These words refer to the 1972 film *Last Tango in Paris*. Another headline in the Sports section of the *Tribune* reads "United against the Center," for an article about how the Chicago Bulls basketball team does not feel comfortable in its new stadium, the United Center. Only a sports fan would immediately know what the headline meant.

Exercise 1. Skimming Headlines for Cultural Values

Newspapers reflect what is important in a country's culture. Below is a list of topics that reflect the concerns of newspaper readers in the United States. Skim a newspaper for headlines that seem to be about the general topic and copy them.

	Topic	Headline
1.	personal finances	
2.	the President's family	
3.	women in politics	
4.	medical news	
5.	clothes and fashion	
6.	personal lives of movie stars	
7.	the importance of dieting	
8.	incomes of famous people	
9.	criticism of a politician	
10.	news of crimes	
11.	problems of minority groups	
12.	advice about personal problems	

Exercise 2. Culture Comparison

Select three topics from those listed above that you would not expect to find in a daily newspaper in your native country. Write the topic and the reason why it would probably not appear.

	Topic	Reason It Would Not Appear
1.		
2.		
3.		

Exercise 3. Behind the Headlines

Now select four of the headlines from Exercise 2. Predict the content of each article from the information in the headline. Then read the article to find its subject. How many of your predictions were accurate? Complete a chart like the one below to show the results.

	Headline	Predicted Subject	Actual Subject
1.			
2.			
3.			
4.			

Exercise 4. Make the Headlines

Cut three articles out of a newspaper. Cut off and save the headlines. With a classmate, trade your cut-off articles. Read the articles you receive and write your own headlines for them. Then compare the headlines you and your partner wrote with the original ones the newspaper printed. In each pair, which headline is better? Why?

Exercise 5. Finding Your Way Around the Newspaper

Look through a newspaper for the information below. Then find the location (the section number and page) where you found each item.

1. the comics
2. an article about a sports event
3. an article about a movie or television program
4. an article about the city or town where you live
5. a "help wanted" job advertisement

The Parts of a Newspaper

U.S. newspapers are organized to help readers find information quickly. Here are some parts of the newspaper that help readers find information:

- **boxes** listing special articles, found on the front page of the paper or of a section
- **an index,** usually found on the first or second page
- **page headings** with the name of the paper, the date, page, and section number
- **headlines and subheadings** that further explain the content of the article

Here are a few specialized newspaper terms that will help you understand the organization of the newspaper:

- **A byline** tells the name of the writer of an article.
- **A caption** explains a photograph and usually appears under it.
- **A column** is a section of print on a page that runs from top to bottom. There are usually four to seven columns on a page.
- **A columnist** is a particular writer whose essay of opinion, or *column,* regularly appears in the newspaper. Sometimes the columnist's picture appears with the article.
- **A dateline** gives the name of the place where the article was written.
- **An editorial** is an essay of opinion by the newspaper editors.
- **A feature article** gives background information about the news and may express the viewpoint of the writer.
- **A lead** is the first paragraph of a news story, and it answers basic factual questions about a news event such as *What occurred? When and where did it happen? Who was involved? What is the significance of the event?* A lead in an article of opinion attempts to arouse readers' interest with intriguing statements.
- **A review** is an article that gives a writer's opinion of a restaurant, film, play, television show, concert, or other form of entertainment.
- **Sections** are the basic divisions of the newspaper, such as national news, local news, business, classified advertisements, and sports. They come in a regular order so readers can find them quickly.

Exercise 5. Identifying Parts of the Newspaper

Look through your local paper (or an English-language newspaper) and cut out five of the items listed above. Look especially for examples of topics, subjects, newspaper parts, or types of articles you wouldn't find in your native country. On a separate sheet of paper, write the headline, part name, or section name for each clipping and the way it is different from what you would find in your native country. With a group of classmates, compare what you have found.

Chicago Tribune

Focus on Culture

Views of Community

Chicago Tribune

Views of Community

People and Community

When people in the United States picture an ideal American community, they might think of the Pilgrims who came over in the seventeenth century. Or they might think of the final scene of the popular film *It's a Wonderful Life*, in which the good-hearted and grateful citizens of a small town get together to save the hero at the film's end. But these two images are ideals that simplify the meaning of community in American culture.

Until the end of the nineteenth century and the beginning of the twentieth, most people in the United States lived on farms. The rural small town was a "close-knit" community, that is, a place where the members all knew each other, helped each other, and shared similar values. With the growth of industry and rail travel, however, people crowded into the cities, and the rural population decreased. New immigrants moved to the cities to work in the factories. Chicago, for example, became a city of many different ethnic neighborhoods, each with its own identity.

The cities grew so large that communities called suburbs sprang up along the city limits. After World War II the suburbs grew in importance as ethnic groups moved out of city neighborhoods and new groups took their place. Some suburbs became known as "bedroom communities" because they seemed to exist only as places for city office workers to sleep before commuting to work each morning.

Today, three main types of communities—rural areas, cities, and suburbs—are in a state of constant change. Rural farming communities fight for their existence as younger people move to the city. People in the city struggle to establish a sense of neighborhood in places where they often feel alone and fear crime—places where they frequently do not even know their neighbors. And the suburbs struggle to remain comfortable places to live while they become more and more crowded and urban as well.

But a community today is more than just people with common interests in the same location. There are other kinds of communities— ones that are not places but groups of people with shared goals. These communities are sometimes even closer than people living on the same block. The pages of the *Chicago Tribune* are filled with references to the "Catholic community," the "business community," the "Mexican community," the "Korean community," or the "homeless community"—groups of people who may be scattered all over the Chicago area but who often know each other better than some next-door neighbors do.

Thus, each person is a member of several communities at the same time, and each community has its own culture, which is constantly changing. This change in turn leads to new communities, many of which eventually become as established as the ones they replace.

Chicago Tribune

Preparation

Inside the 'Pilsen/Little Village' exhibit

Previewing the Article

What is a neighborhood?

For Chicago artist Marcos Raya, it is more than a city area with specific boundaries and people. For him it is a place with a past that he is proud to think of as his own. Written about a Chicago Historical Society exhibit on a historic Chicago area, this article tells of a Mexican immigrant who feels a special bond with the previous residents of his neighborhood. That bond is the working class struggle that has been enacted in his neighborhood since the arrival of some of the earliest European immigrants to the Chicago area.

Pilsen/Little Village has long been a vital cultural and economic crossroads. From the mid-nineteenth century through the middle of the twentieth, people from Ireland, Germany, Poland, Croatia, Lithuania, Italy, and especially Bohemia (now the Czech Republic) used the area as a point of entry to life in the United States and, in doing so, left their mark. And for at least the last thirty years, Mexican immigrants have been the dominant group. All of these groups have struggled: the earlier European groups struggled for workers' rights and unions, and the Mexicans fought for educational reform, political representation, and social justice. And through these struggles they have helped shape the culture of the United States.

Before You Read

Discuss the following questions:

1. What is a muralist? Where can you see murals? Describe some murals you have seen.
2. The famous Haymarket Riot grew out of a labor dispute involving workers in the Pilsen neighborhood in 1886. What do you know about the Haymarket Riot? Look up a brief description in an encyclopedia.
3. How can the arts be used as a means of social protest? Give some examples.

As You Read

Look for these main ideas:

1. Why does Marcos Raya love his neighborhood?
2. How can social class—here the working class—be a link between ethnic groups?

Inside the
'Pilsen/Little Village'
exhibit

By Jay Pridmore
TRIBUNE STAFF WRITER

1 Pilsen, says muralist Marcos Raya, is a place of struggle, and now that Raya has overcome personal demons in his life and his art, he has a new battle on his mind.

2 "People want to change the character of 18th Street. They want to put up pseudo-California buildings . . . colonial . . . adobe. But it's not Pilsen."

3 Raya, a Chicagoan for more than 25 years, wants to save the old European architecture of the street. He wants ample room for murals, of course, but he has come to love the old German and Bohemian buildings that make Pilsen one of Chicago's most antique neighborhoods.

4 The artist was visiting a new exhibit about his neighborhood at the Chicago Historical Society, entitled "Pilsen/Little Village: Our Home, Our Struggle." Raya admitted he's no expert on the history of the neighborhood, which included Czechs and Polish a half-century ago, and Germans and Irish before that.

5 But the artist, who contributed a large canvas mural to the exhibit, is intrigued by the long line of ethnic groups that have occupied the area just south and west of the Loop. To Raya, the neighborhood is infinitely complex.

6 "Pilsen isn't Mexico," he said. "It is a completely different reality."

7 Sorting out that reality was the objective of curators of the Historical Society exhibit, which runs until May 11, 1997. They discovered, naturally, that connections with the past are sometimes faint. But some links remain. The most important is Pilsen's working-class character.

8 Ever since the earliest days in Chicago, factories were built around the river and canal, Chicago's first major trade route. Where factories were concentrated, labor struggles were inevitable, and many of those struggles are chronicled in the exhibit.

9 Years ago, for example, there was the McCormick Reaper Works, where thousands of European workers found jobs and also got involved in a series of famous strikes. Labor activism led to political power. In the 1920s, Czech immigrant Anton Cermak began in factories and built what became the Democratic political organization; Cermak was elected mayor of Chicago in 1931. More recently, Pilsen has fought on behalf of recent immigrants and undocumented workers, most of them from Mexico.

Cafe Jumping Bean, 1439 W. 18th St., is a neighborhood institution in Pilsen/Little Village. Owner Eleazar Delgado is shown outside on the steps.
Photo courtesy of the Chicago Historical Society.

10   The wide-ranging exhibit also chronicles a long arts tradition. In Czech days, fine arts and performing arts were central to life in Pilsen, named for a famous beer-making city in Bohemia. Today in Pilsen, the arts primarily means murals, painted by local artists, some of whom have national reputations. An important art museum has been established there, where works by Posada, Rivera and other Mexican luminaries have been shown.

11   For his part, Marcos Raya sees himself naturally in the image of Rivera, who painted colorful murals on topics with social impact. But he sees himself not just in political terms; Raya's also affected by more personal things.

12   There's Kim Novak, for instance. As a youngster in Irapuato, Mexico, Raya saw her movies and became a bit infatuated with her. Only later, after he moved to Chicago, did he learn that the actress herself came from Pilsen.

13   Now, he says, at least half-seriously, that he wants to build a monument to her in the neighborhood. It would be one of Raya's less political works of art. But it might make the artist, now a Chicagoan through and through, feel just a little more at home in Pilsen.

14   "Pilsen/Little Village: Our Home, Our Struggle" continues through May 11, 1997, at the Chicago Historical Society, Clark Street and North Avenue. Museum hours are 9:30 A.M. to 4:30 P.M. Monday through Saturday, and noon to 5 P.M. Sundays. Admission is $3 for adults, $2 for seniors and students, and $1 for children (6–16); 312-642-4600.

Chicago Tribune

Postreading

I. Getting the Message

After reading the article, choose the best answer for each item.

1. Marcos Raya thinks that some of the new architecture that is planned for Pilsen
   a. is good because it reflects the current Mexican immigrant population.
   b. is not good because it does not reflect Pilsen's heritage.
   c. is good because it is beautiful.

2. Marcos Raya thinks that his neighborhood
   a. needs a great deal of improvement.
   b. has too many old and out-of-date buildings.
   c. is interesting because it has a rich history.

3. Even though many ethnic groups have lived in Pilsen over the years, one aspect that has remained the same is that
   a. it has always been working class.
   b. it has always been a peaceful place.
   c. it has never been politically important.

4. According to the article, one of Pilsen's current political issues is
   a. the pollution of the Chicago River.
   b. the problems of recent immigrants.
   c. the rights of artists.

5. Marcos Raya thinks of himself mainly as an artist who
   a. communicates a political and social message.
   b. avoids politics.
   c. is trying to widen the influence of Mexican culture on the art of Pilsen.

6. Raya's interest in building a monument to the actress Kim Novak shows
   a. that there is a personal dimension to his art.
   b. that he is knowledgeable about film.
   c. that he is not a serious artist.

Check your answers with the key on page 165. If you have made mistakes, reread the article to gain a better understanding of it.

Chicago Tribune

Postreading

II. Expanding Your Vocabulary

A. Getting Meaning from Context

Find each word in the paragraph indicated in parentheses. Use context clues to determine the meaning of the word. Then choose the best definition.

1. ample (3)   a. less   b. enough
2. intrigued (5)   a. interested   b. offended
3. complex (5)   a. complicated   b. boring
4. curators (7)   a. artists showing   b. people in charge of
                         their work   a museum
5. faint (7)   a. weak   b. active
6. inevitable (8)   a. violent   b. certain to happen
7. chronicles (10)   a. sells   b. tells the history of
8. luminaries (10)   a. famous people   b. unimportant people
9. infatuated (12)   a. interested in   b. in love with

B. Practicing Useful Vocabulary

Complete the sentences below with words from exercise A.

1. In order to exhibit a large mural, the museum curators had to make sure they had _____

   space.

2. The working-class character of Pilsen is one connection with the neighborhood's past that is not

   _____ .

3. Pilsen is _____ because many different groups of people have lived in it over the years.

4. In Pilsen one can visit a museum that sometimes exhibits work by _____ of Mexican art.

Chicago Tribune

Postreading

III. Making Sense of Sentences

Find each phrase in the paragraph indicated in parentheses. Read the whole paragraph. Then choose the statement that best conveys the meaning of the phrase.

1. personal demons (1)
    a. Raya had to overcome superstitious beliefs.
    b. Raya had to overcome serious personal problems.
2. most antique neighborhoods (3)
    a. Pilsen is an old and interesting area.
    b. Pilsen has excellent antique shops.
3. long line of ethnic groups (5)
    a. Many different ethnic groups live there today.
    b. Many different ethnic groups have lived there over a period of time.
4. wide-ranging exhibit (10)
    a. The exhibit is very large.
    b. The exhibit has many diverse aspects.
5. central to life (10)
    a. The arts were centrally located in the area.
    b. The arts were very important.
6. in the image of Rivera (11)
    a. Raya's paintings are imitations of Rivera's.
    b. Raya has the same artistic purpose as Rivera.
7. topics with social impact (11)
    a. The murals have social and political themes.
    b. The murals have made a big impact on society.
8. at least half-seriously (13)
    a. Raya is not serious about building a monument to Kim Novak.
    b. Raya is attracted to the idea of building a monument to Kim Novak.

IV. Talking and Writing

Discuss the following topics. Then choose one of them to write about.

1. The author of the article mentions that Raya himself has a large canvas mural in the exhibit. Why doesn't the author describe the mural?
2. In your native city are there neighborhoods that have been occupied by several different ethnic groups over the years? Are current residents aware of the past communities that have lived there?
3. What do you know about the neighborhood you live in now? Is it populated by one main national group? How has its population changed in the last hundred years?
4. Do you think it is a good thing for people from one national group to live together and even dominate a neighborhood? What are the advantages of this? What are the disadvantages?

Chicago Tribune

Preparation

Do names come naturally?

Previewing the Article

People enjoy naming places. From the time of the first European settlers through wave upon wave of immigrants pushing west, new places were created—states, cities, villages, farms—and all of them had to be named. It was a marvelous new privilege for people coming from countries where the towns and cities had had their names for many hundreds of years. The ability to name a new town suited a developing New World culture that valued the idea that an individual or a family could remake itself and throw off the limitations of the Old World.

This article is about how the habit of naming continues today, even if in some rather strange forms. New suburbs, new subdivisions, and new streets are named with great enthusiasm and hard financial calculation. But there is a current style of naming that encourages home buyers to imagine that they are living in a more colorful world. As the writer of the article notes, "Home buyers aren't looking to replicate their actual roots, but link into a past of their preference." This insistence on the individual's freedom to create a new reality, even a new "past," connects today's home buyers to the earliest settlers.

The following definitions will help you read the article with greater understanding:

* A *development* is a large group of houses of similar design constructed and sold by a *developer*.
* *Levittown* is a famous housing development on Long Island, New York, of low-cost homes built for World War II veterans between 1946 and 1951.
* An *Anglophile* is a person who admires England and English culture.
* James Madison (1761–1836) was a U.S. president, orator, and writer.

Before You Read

Discuss the following questions:
1. Read the headline. How could a name "come naturally"?
2. Read the tag line (below the headline). What is the double meaning of "concrete"?
3. Look at a map of the United States. Can you guess the origin of some of the city and state names? Which ones?

As You Read

As you read, look for the three different kinds of place names that have been popular in the United States. Which kind is currently most popular?

Do names come naturally?

We're lured by images of peaceful woods even if the reality is concrete crossroads

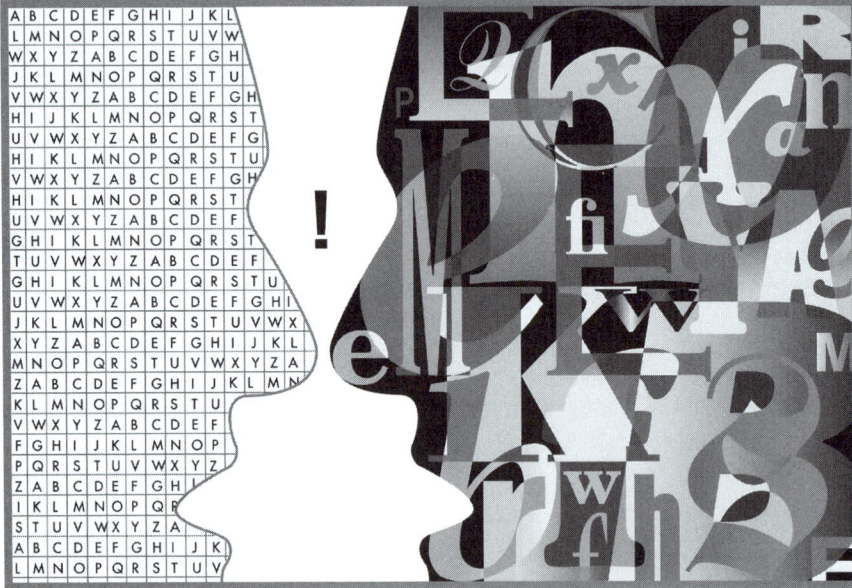

Illustration by Frank Collyer/SIS

By T. J. Becker
SPECIAL TO THE TRIBUNE

1 "What's in a name?" asks Shakespeare's love-stricken Juliet, pointing out that "a rose by any other word would smell as sweet."

2 But when it comes to marketing real estate, today's developers aren't content with any old epithet.

3 Our streets and communities once were named in memory of founding fathers or to reflect geographic features. Today, however, appellation of place—known as toponymy in linguistic circles—is a marketing exercise aimed at pushing consumer hot buttons.

4 "Image mongering," the deliberate fashioning of names to sell, is not a new phenomenon, says Wilbur Zelinsky, professor emeritus of geography at Penn State University. But, he adds, the practice has accelerated in recent years: "Society is increasingly commercial and concerned with the bottom line. The intensity (of image mongering) is accelerating as we're obsessed with trying to stay afloat economically."

5 During the early chapters of U.S. history when political ideology and national fever were running high, names of places (and people) frequently were drawn from ancient Greece and Rome. After World War II, developments often were named after their founder or his family, such as Levittown.

6 Names might also be devised to establish a link with a nearby community: a subdivision near Libertyville might be christened Libertyville Acres or Libertyville Heights.

7 "Today we're completely away from that," says Edward Callary, an English professor at Northern Illinois University in DeKalb. For the last five years, Callary has been tracking development names around the Chicago area, compiling a database to chart trends.

8 "Place names are no longer commemorative or descriptive," he says. "They are evocative."

9 Indeed, while consumer products exploit sex, real estate names tap into lifestyle yearnings and aspirations.

10 Old World tradition is big, particularly when it features an English accent. Among today's home buyers there appear to be a great many Anglophiles who warm up to names like Chelsea Meadows and Foxtail Glen, say name experts.

11 Other nations, however, are largely overlooked when it comes to coining names for residential real estate. There is a smattering of Scottish and a little French, but no German, no Italian, no Polish. For the Chicago area, Callary reports only one or two Hispanic names listed in his database.

12   Home buyers aren't looking to replicate their actual roots, but link into a past of their preference, says Callary: "People buy an image that never was . . . we're trying to create a mythic past."

13   If a name doesn't sound antique enough, namesmiths enhance its charm, adding an "e" (Towne or Pointe) for a bit of extra patina.

14   Some more appellative irony: 30 years ago, consumers were looking for urban polish. Today, they're seeking rural roots; everyone wants to be a gentleman farmer. And developers aim to please, devising names like Country Walk, Autumn Meadows, or Bramblewood Oaks.

15   "Perhaps the most painful irony of suburban real estate development is a nomenclature given to evoking the natural environment and countryside which it obliterates," observes Darrell Norris, a professor of geography at State University of New York in Geneseo, who refers to the result as "unreal estate."

16   When Norris studied new housing developments in Rochester, N.Y., he discovered almost two-thirds of all name elements used in advertisments fostered images of nature or rural living—"woods," "meadows," "brook" and "creek" being among the most prominent.

17   But a little water seems to go a long way. Norris found the words "stream" and "river" were avoided by developers, who perhaps feared consumers would associate these terms with flooding.

18   Contradiction runs rampant in contemporary place naming. Callary points to Lakewood Falls, a development near southwest suburban Plainfield. Despite its name, there is no lake, no woods and no falls. Unusual hybrids also crop up: "Hickory Oaks."

19   Pushing the envelope even more, townhouse communities often incorporate "manor" or "chateau" in their titles—terms that evoke images of grand single family houses rather than medium-density developments.

20   Even streets can't seem to escape embellishment. In today's subdivisions, homeowners don't just live on a street or avenue, they dwell on a circle, court, lane, place, way or mew.

21   Whereas real estate names once evolved slowly, little is left to chance. Today names are devised before a shovelful of dirt has turned for a development.

22   "Place naming has become a deadly serious business," says Callary. Referring to a Chicago development originally dubbed "Sherlock Homes," Callary notes the houses sold poorly at first, causing the developer to change the name to something less whimsical.

23   While deliberate humor may be absent, there are attempts to wax poetic. Zelinsky points to streets in Columbia, Md., with "gem-like mini-haiku names": Spring Step, Sleep Soft Circle, Moon Portrait Way, Mossy Brink, Wind Dance Way, Perfect Hour.

24   Ironically, for all the effort, the psychological impact of place names is short-lived.

25   "When you hear a name for the first time, it's bound to incite some kind of excitement. But the name quickly becomes opaque," says Zelinsky.

26   The historical relevance of most place names is taken for granted today, says Zelinsky. Neither Madison, Wis., nor Madison Avenue conjure up the image of James Madison. And it's doubtful that residents of Cicero give much thought to their Roman statesman namesake.

27   "The name acquires a life of its own," says Zelinsky. Yet it's a different story with personal names, which do have lasting impact on behavior.

28   There may be some shifts ahead in place naming, as real estate marketers encounter more niches.

29   "The kinds of strategies that used to work well may not be as effective as they were in the past. Group identification is much more complex than it used to be," says Norris, suggesting place naming might become more narrowly cast.

30   Fortunately, developers have a lot of leeway with labels. Natural features appearing on federal maps must be approved by the U.S. Board on Geographic Names, but community names usually are approved at the county level. (If a dispute can't be handled at the local or state level, then the federal Board on Geographic Names may get involved, says Roger Payne, executive secretary of the Reston, Va.-based agency.)

31   Nor are place names permanent. Many disparaging names like Cripple Creek or Negro Mountain are being changed to something more palatable. But more often, names are altered for commercial reasons than for reasons of political correctness.

32   Stateline, a community straddling the California-Nevada border near Lake Tahoe, tried to assume the name of the well-known lake a few years ago. The idea was quashed quickly by other resort communities nearby which didn't want to be left out in the cold, reports Payne.

33   Last summer a group in northwest suburban Carpentersville unsuccessfully proposed changing the community name to Dundee; the village is located between East Dundee and West Dundee and the faction felt this would be a more appropriate image than the community's current name.

34   The psychological impact of place names may be short-lived, but not while change is in the air, says Payne: "You've got a highly emotional situation on your hands."

35   Payne recalls stories of board members having their lives threatened over name alterations. Nothing quite so menacing has happened to him, but he adds, "I've had numerous people in tears and some bitter complaining."

Postreading

Chicago Tribune

I. Getting the Message

After you read the article, indicate if each statement below is true (T) or false (F).

1. _____ The right name can help sell a new housing development.
2. _____ In the early history of the United States, places were sometimes named after people and places in ancient Greece and Rome.
3. _____ Many names currently chosen for real estate developments are taken from famous people in American history.
4. _____ English-sounding names are very popular in real estate today.
5. _____ Home buyers today do not like images of rural life or nature in the name of a development.
6. _____ Home buyers today prefer names that reflect places in their native countries or countries of their ancestors.
7. _____ The psychological effect of place names lasts for many years.
8. _____ When names are changed, it is often for commercial reasons.
9. _____ People have strong feelings about changing the name of a place.

Check your answers with the key on page 165. If you have made mistakes, reread the article to gain a better understanding of it.

II. Expanding Your Vocabulary

A. Getting Meaning from Context
Find each word in the paragraph indicated in parentheses. Use context clues to determine the meaning of the word. Choose the best definition.

1. obsessed (4)   a. very concerned   b. tired, weary
2. ideology (5)   a. political philosophy   b. religious belief
3. yearnings (9)   a. demands   b. strong desires
4. enhance (13)   a. increase   b. limit
5. obliterates (15)   a. re-creates   b. destroys completely
6. fostered (16)   a. named   b. promoted
7. mew (20)   a. a kind of street   b. a kind of suburb
8. alterations (35)   a. selling points   b. changes
9. menacing (35)   a. important   b. threatening

B. Reading for Suggested Meanings
Answer these questions. For help, reread the indicated paragraphs.

1. A *hybrid* (18) is a plant or animal produced from parents of different breeds. The word can also be used figuratively to indicate a strange result. Is "Hickory Oaks" a literal or figurative hybrid?
2. *Homes* (22) in "Sherlock Homes" refers to Sherlock *Holmes*, the famous English detective in the stories of Arthur Conan Doyle. Why did this name fail to appeal to homeowners?

Chicago Tribune

Postreading

III. Working with Idioms and Expressions

Study the meaning of the following idioms and expressions.

pushing consumer hot buttons (3) appealing to the strongest desires of buyers

stay afloat economically (4) be free of financial trouble

running high (5) very strong, in an excited state

tap into (9) gain access to

warm up to (10) begin to like or be interested in

pushing the envelope (19) going to the limit or stretching the limit

taken for granted (26) treated in an indifferent manner

have a lot of leeway (30) have a lot of freedom of action

Now answer these questions.
1. Why are the weeks before Christmas an important time for advertisers to *push consumer hot buttons?*
2. What should a person with a small income do to *stay afloat economically?*
3. In your native country, on what occasions are political feelings *running high?*
4. Are there any sports that are not popular in your native country that you have begun to *warm up to?*
5. Why are famous tourist attractions often *taken for granted* by the people who live near them?
6. Do you think children need to *have a lot of leeway* while they are growing up?

IV. Talking and Writing

Discuss the topics below. Then choose one of them to write about.
1. What is the origin of the name of the city or town you now live in? your street? your college?
2. The author says that place names start out with a certain meaning but soon take on a life of their own. An example would be Washington, D.C. Though the city was named after George Washington, people do not generally think of the first president when they hear the name of the city. The author adds, "Yet it's a different story with personal names, which do have a lasting impact on behavior." What does this last statement mean? What examples can you think of that would illustrate this point?

Chicago Tribune

Focus on Culture

Setting the Scene

Daily newspapers serve the local community and all the smaller communities that live within it. The *Chicago Tribune*, for example, contains news about neighborhoods, many of which are populated by ethnic communities, such as those of Chicago's Poles, Greeks, Mexicans, and Ukrainians. It also covers news about the suburban and rural communities surrounding the city. Finally, it serves other communities scattered all over the city, such the homeless and organized labor. Some communities, also known as "interest groups" because of their shared interests, work for political change favorable to their groups.

Stories about the issues faced by various communities can be found in almost every section of a daily newspaper.

- **National News Section.** National news is often supplied by a national wire service such as the Associated Press. Immigration law, court cases involving discrimination, and education and welfare legislation are just a few of the issues in the news that cause strong reactions in local communities.
- **Local News Section.** Large newspapers such as the *Chicago Tribune* have separate editions in different areas that each devote an entire section to local community news. This section contains news stories and feature stories of interest to neighborhoods and special groups. News stories report the facts but do not give a writer's personal point of view; most of the important information comes at the beginning and answers the key questions *who, what, where, when, why,* and *how.*
- **Features Section.** The *Tribune*'s features section is called "Tempo." Other newspapers' features sections have names like "Lifestyles" or simply "Features." These contain stories that explain, interpret, or give background information on the issues in the news. Feature stories can be found in almost any other section of the newspaper, even on the front page.
- **Editorial and Opinion Pages.** Editorials are short essays that express the opinions of the newspaper's editorial board and other journalists who write for the paper. When news of importance happens in a specific community, readers like to find out a newspaper's official opinion about it. For example, if a university wants to expand into a particular neighborhood and the community members object, the newspaper is likely to express a point of view about the issue. Editorials are usually found toward the back of the paper's first section.
- **Letters to the Editor.** These are short essays of opinion written by readers in reaction to stories in the newspaper. They are usually found next to the editorials. Quite often leaders of community groups write letters to the editor expressing agreement or disagreement with stories published in the newspaper.
- **Columns.** Throughout the newspaper and on the page opposite the editorials there are essays by individual writers called columnists. Columnists are frequently engaged in community issues and are sometimes identified with the specific problems of certain groups.

Chicago Tribune

Focus on Culture

Exercise 1. The Newspaper and the Communities it Serves

These are some of the communities that newspapers contain stories about. Some of these terms are often followed by the word *community;* others are interest groups united by common concerns.

neighborhoods	national or ethnic groups
suburbs	minority groups
small towns	women
geographic areas	the homeless
business	labor
education	disabled
elderly	welfare
defense or military	health care
particular religious faiths	single parents

In this exercise find articles from a newspaper about some of the communities above. On a separate sheet of paper, complete a chart like the one below. In the first column, write the name of the community that is mentioned in the article. In the next two columns, write the headline and the section of the newspaper in which you found the article. Then check whether the article reports a news event or whether it is commentary in the form of a feature or opinion column. If you can find articles about other local communities not mentioned above, include them in the chart.

	Name of Community	Headline of Article	Section of Newspaper	News	Feature or Opinion
1.					
2.					
3.					
4.					
5.					
6.					
7.					
8.					

Focus on Culture

Exercise 2. The News in Depth

Choose a news article from your list on page 15. Read the article carefully. Then analyze it by answering the questions below.

1. Who wrote the article? In what city and state did the story originate?
2. Does the article answer the six key questions—*who, what, where, when, why,* and *how*—in the first few paragraphs? What are the answers?
3. Does the article include all the information you want to know about the topic? If not, what is missing?
4. Does a photo or illustration accompany the article? If so, what information does it provide? Does it help the reader understand the main point of the article?
5. Does the information in this article differ in any way from what you heard on the radio, saw on television, or read in another newspaper about the same event? If so, what do you think is the reason for the difference?
6. Could such an article appear in your local newspaper in your native country? Is the community affected in this article similar to a community in your native country? How is this community viewed?

Exercise 3. The Feature or Opinion Article in Depth

Select a feature or opinion article from those in exercise 1. After reading it carefully, analyze the story by answering the questions below.

1. What is the community discussed in the story? What is the author's attitude toward this community? Is the author mainly describing an interesting aspect of this group, or is the author trying to persuade the reader to think differently about this group?
2. Does this article explain something you didn't know before about the way people live in the United States? If so, describe it.
3. Does the community described in the article exist in your native country? If so, what is the attitude toward this community?

Exercise 4. Writing a Journal: Your Community

What community or communities do you belong to in the United States? Many people belong to more than one. To use a Chicago example, a Roman Catholic nurse from Mexico might be said to belong to the Pilsen Community, the Catholic community, the Hispanic community, and the health-care community, among others. Write down the various communities you belong to. Then, in reading the daily newspaper, find one article each day that contains elements that relate to you. In a brief entry for each day, take these notes:

1. Write down the title and author of the article.
2. Summarize in a few sentences the main idea of the article.
3. Write your opinion of the article in one or two sentences. Did you like it? Did it give you any new information about the culture of the United States?

Chicago Tribune

The World of Business and Work

1
Cubicle, sweet cubicle

2
Companies that still make people—not profit—top priority

Focus on Culture

The World of Business and Work

Chicago Tribune

The World of Business and Work

The Place of Business and Work in U.S. Society

Henry Ford, the famous U.S. inventor and car manufacturer, once said, "The business of America is business." By this he meant that the U.S. way of life is based on the values of the business world.

Few would argue with Ford's statement. A brief glimpse at a daily newspaper vividly shows how much people in the United States think about business. For example, nearly every newspaper has a business section, in which the deals and projects, finances and management, stock prices and labor problems of corporations are reported daily. In addition, business news can appear in every other section. Most national news has an important financial aspect to it. Welfare, foreign aid, the federal budget, and the policies of the Federal Reserve Bank are all heavily affected by business. Moreover, business news appears in some of the unlikeliest places. The world of arts and entertainment is often referred to as "the entertainment industry" or "show business." Many readers are just as interested in how much money movie stars earn in a film as they are in their performances.

The positive side of Henry Ford's statement can be seen in the prosperity that business has brought to U.S. life. One of the most important reasons so many people from all over the world come to live in the United States is the dream of a better job. Jobs are produced in abundance because the U.S. economic system—often referred to as the "free market" system—is driven by competition and not by government planning. People believe that this system creates more wealth, more jobs, and a materially better way of life for most of the population.

The negative side of Henry Ford's statement, however, can be seen when the word *business* is taken to mean *big business*. And the term *big business*—referring to the biggest companies, such as the oil, railroad, steel, mining, automobile, and communications corporations—is seen in opposition to *labor*. Throughout U.S. history working people have had to fight hard for higher wages, better working conditions, and the right to form unions. Today, many of the old labor disputes are over, but there is still some employee anxiety. *Downsizing*—a word meaning the laying off of thousands of workers to keep expenses low and profits high—is a term that creates feelings of insecurity for many.

Business is such a dominant element in the culture of the United States that many business values—such as hard work, competition, individualism, and teamwork—are expected parts of everyday social life.

Chicago Tribune

Preparation

Cubicle, sweet cubicle

Previewing the Article

The old expression is "Home, Sweet Home" because home is a place to relax and be yourself.

Thus, the title of this article—"Cubicle, sweet cubicle"—is a joke, for "relaxing" and "being yourself" would be big mistakes—if not simply impossible—for anybody working in one of these tiny, doorless, low-walled offices. In their box-like sameness, cubicles tend to offend people in the United States who value *individualism*. This cultural ideal, that people should be able to have independent, separate, and proud identities, was nurtured in the small, isolated farms of the first European settlers in America. These immigrants sought freedom, and individualism was one important result of their search.

When most people worked on farms, the space they had to work in was very large. But as more and more people started to work in mines, factories, and offices, and as people began to live in small houses and apartments, they found that the ideal of individualism was harder to reach.

This article addresses two questions raised by the arrangement of work space in the modern office: (1) How can a person working in a cubicle create and maintain a feeling of individuality? and (2) What informal rules of behavior develop in the small culture, or *subculture,* of the modern office?

Before You Read

Discuss these questions.

1. Have you ever worked in a cubicle? How did you feel about it? If you have never worked in one, do you think you would like to?
2. The subtitle of the article is "Learning to thrive in a beehive." What does this mean? *To thrive* means "to be successful." What is a beehive? How does it resemble an office full of cubicles?
3. Do newspapers in your native country contain articles that give readers advice? What kinds of subjects do these articles discuss?

As You Read

The article gives readers a great deal of advice on how to establish and keep their individuality in an office environment. Find four of the suggestions that the article gives.

Cubicle,
sweet cubicle

Learning to thrive in a beehive

By Michele Weldon
SPECIAL TO THE TRIBUNE

1   Very few employees get the corner office with the panoramic skyline view anymore. What's more likely to happen is we sink into tiny, homogeneous cubicles every morning. Some even toil in offices embracing "hoteling," in which workers have only temporary claim to a desk or work area on a first-come, first-served basis.

2   "In a cubicle environment, it is much more difficult. Status gets mowed down. The uniformity takes away a person's uniqueness. There is this openness with no privacy which is a limitation of sanctuary," says Dan Conti, a psychologist and director of the employee assistance program at First Chicago NBD Corp.

3   How can you do your job well in these privacy-impaired work spaces and still feel comfortable and productive?

4   Working at tuning out the surrounding noises and intensely focusing on the task at hand works for some. "The best source of distraction is pouring yourself into your work," says Conti.

5   "I would not focus on the cubicle, I would focus on the work," agrees Marsha Sinetar, author of "To Build The Life You Want, Create The Work You Love: The Spiritual Domain of Entrepreneuring" (St. Martin's/Griffin, $9.95) and president and founder of Sinetar Associates, in Santa Rosa, Calif., specializing in strategic planning, marketing and leadership consulting.

6   In a beehive existence, the lack of a privacy zone where you can concentrate and de-stress without public scrutiny presents a substantial challenge. The relentless exposure to others' chatter and personal and professional business

DILBERT ® by Scott Adams

DILBERT reprinted by permission of United Feature Syndicate, Inc.

also is draining. Conti recommends brief breaks, whether to lunch with non-work friends, walk around the office or stroll outside, to supply some mental respite.

7   A code of cubicle conduct also can help you and your open-space neighbors coexist harmoniously. Keep your voice moderated and accord others at least the illusion of privacy by not jumping into conversations or responding to what you've heard them speak about on the phone. Also, respect boundaries by sending others electronic messages when appropriate instead of constantly intruding on their area.

8   To remind yourself of your roles outside the work environment, include photographs of your family or your favorite rose garden on your desk. Also, a "simple splash of humor" via cartoons or sayings in your cubicle can help keep your work life in perspective.

9   Design experts say there are also simple ways to make your work space more appealing. "The more pleasing, the more organized and the more aesthetic (your

space) is, the more together you're going to be," says Celeste Cooper, creative director of Repertoire, a design firm with offices in Boston and New York. For example, improving your "deskscape" with black-and-white desk accessories and a framed black-and-white photograph can help your attitude as well as neutralize the impact of an odious cubicle color, Cooper says.

10   A low level of clutter also counts. "People tend to have clearer thoughts when it is all in order," says Rita Falkner, president of FSI of New York Ltd., a design firm.

11   Eclectic and interesting desk accessories such as handmade pottery can infuse style, says Trina Catania, owner of Catania Executive Gifts, a gift company in Chicago.

12   Yet overdoing the decorating in your cubicle can be as big a problem as having an anonymous, lifeless spot. It is inappropriate to

exceed your space with plants or large frames that rise above the top or exceed the width of your cubicle. Resist the urge to fill every square inch with a personal memento. "Every office needs 'rest walls' or blank spaces to look at," says Linda Marder, principal in her own design firm in Los Angeles.

13   After a full day of working in your cubicle or desk in an open area, Conti says, it is imperative to recuperate from a sense of always "being in the middle of it," with time spent alone in your home.

14   The proper attitude is also important, Sinetar advises. "If working in a cubicle is your biggest problem, then you are blessed."

Chicago Tribune

Postreading

I. Getting the Message .

After reading the article, indicate if each statement is true (T) or false (F).

1. _____ This article mainly gives advice to the reader about working in a cubicle.
2. _____ The article contains fascinating information about the history of cubicle use.
3. _____ One of the main problems is that office workers find concentration difficult in cubicles because of the lack of privacy.
4. _____ One of the suggestions for better concentration is to play music on a radio so that the worker can't hear other people speak.
5. _____ Some experts say that an organized and attractive desk area helps a person think clearly.
6. _____ One informal rule of cubicle conduct is that one should not speak about others' telephone conversations.
7. _____ Photographs of one's family and some personal decorating help an office worker feel more comfortable in a cubicle.
8. _____ Office workers should visit each other's cubicles frequently so they can stay alert and won't feel sleepy.

Check your answers with the key on page 165. If you have made mistakes, reread the article to gain a better understanding of it.

II. Expanding Your Vocabulary

A. Getting Meaning from Context

Find each word or phrase in the paragraph indicated in parentheses. Use context clues to determine the meaning of the word or phrase. Then choose the best definition.

1. homogeneous (1)   a. the same   b. beautiful
2. toil (1)   a. sit   b. work
3. domain (5)   a. area   b. problem
4. substantial (6)   a. big   b. unimportant
5. harmoniously (7)   a. stressfully   b. peacefully
6. moderated (7)   a. not loud   b. not political
7. odious (9)   a. dark   b. ugly
8. imperative (13)   a. necessary   b. unwise

Postreading

B. Defining Useful Vocabulary

Match each word with its definition.

1. _____ uniformity (2)   a. safe, protected situation
2. _____ sanctuary (2)   b. showing a sense of beauty
3. _____ stroll (6)   c. disorder, mess
4. _____ aesthetic (9)   d. sameness
5. _____ clutter (10)   e. put in
6. _____ infuse (11)   f. walk in a relaxed way

C. Practicing Useful Vocabulary

Complete the sentences with words from the left column of exercise B.

1. Since cubicles in an office all look exactly alike, the _____ of the work spaces can seem boring.

2. Too much _____ on any desk can slow down a person's ability to work quickly.

3. A typical office cubicle is usually not very _____ because it is made for work, not for anyone's

   personal idea of beauty.

4. A cubicle doesn't provide the personal _____ that an actual office does.

III. Working with Idioms and Expressions

Study the meanings of the idioms and expressions below. A form of each one appears
in the article in the paragraph indicated in parentheses.

sink into (1) stay and become very involved
first-come, first-served basis (1) arranged or done in the order that people arrive
mowed down (2) cut down
tuning out (4) ignoring
task at hand (4) work that must be done immediately
pour yourself into (4) work very hard and enthusiastically
code of conduct (7) an informal set of rules for behavior
jumping into (7) quickly and thoughtlessly joining an activity
keep in perspective (8) know what is really important in life
together (9) emotionally healthy and well-organized
be in the middle of it (13) be very involved in busy activity

Chicago Tribune

Postreading

Complete these sentences with the idioms and expressions from page 23.

1. Because a cubicle has no ceiling or door, a worker sometimes finds that _____ office noise is difficult.

2. A _____ is necessary in an office so that workers do not bother each other.

3. Since work is only one part of a person's life, it is important to _____ the problems that develop at the office.

4. A happy, _____ person can get more work done than a disorganized, unhappy person.

IV. Analyzing Paragraphs

Answer these questions about the article.
1. In paragraph 1, which of the following does the author suggest?
   a. Office workers have always worked in cubicles.
   b. Years ago more workers had personal offices.
2. What does the quotation from the psychologist in paragraph 2 indicate?
   a. Americans do not feel a need for privacy at work.
   b. Americans do not like the sameness of cubicles.
3. Paragraph 7 gives rules for maintaining a pleasant work environment. What do these rules mainly deal with?
   a. They tell how and when to communicate with others at work.
   b. They tell how to deal with rude co-workers.
4. How many authorities are mentioned or quoted in paragraphs 9–12?
   a. Four are mentioned.
   b. Three are mentioned.
5. What does the quotation from Marsha Sinetar in paragraph 14 suggest?
   a. Unhappiness with working in a cubicle is a small problem.
   b. Cubicles are terrible places for people to work.

V. Talking and Writing

Discuss the following topics. Then choose one of them to write about.
1. Do people from your own culture feel as uncomfortable working in cubicles as Americans do? Why or why not?
2. This article discusses unwritten rules that people develop wherever they meet regularly. What unwritten rules are there for behavior and speech in an American college classroom?
3. Can you think of several work environments that you regard as *worse* than cubicles? What makes them worse?

Chicago Tribune

Preparation

Companies that still make people—not profit—top priority

Previewing the Article

"I'm a company man." This was something many workers in the United States were accustomed to saying with pride for most of this century. It meant that the worker was proud of working for a particular company throughout adulthood. Both *blue collar* (or manufacturing) workers and *white collar* (or office) workers often felt loyal to a company—and the company returned this loyalty. But since the loss of thousands of manufacturing jobs in the 1960s and 1970s and of thousands more white collar jobs in the 1980s and 1990s, this expression has become a mere memory. In the late 1990s employees feel it is foolish to be loyal to a company that could fire them at any moment.

This article is about a change in this atmosphere of mistrust. Many companies, the writer reports, are beginning to realize that a worried, insecure employee is not a productive one and that it makes sense for a company to create a happy workplace. Companies are starting to creatively use *fringe benefits*—benefits other than straight salary—to make employees feel valued and even foster a family atmosphere at the workplace.

Before You Read

Discuss these questions.

1. Read the headline. What does *top priority* mean? Most companies make profits the top priority. Why?
2. Have you, or others you know, ever worked for a company with many fringe benefits? What sort of benefits were offered? Do you think a person should ask about fringe benefits in a job interview?
3. When people in your native country first go to work for an employer, do they expect to work for that employer for the rest of their lives?
4. Have you ever worked for an employer who made you feel loyal to the company? How did the employer foster this feeling?

As You Read

Look for the two main sources of written information that the writer relied on for this story.

Companies that still make people—not profit—top priority

Carol Kleiman

1 Workers at the Wilton Conner Packaging Co. in Charlotte, N.C., get their laundry done on the premises for $1 a load.

2 Federal Express Corp. in Memphis names planes for employees' children.

3 Silicon Graphics Inc. of Mountain View, Calif., allows water fights at the end of major projects.

4 John Nuveen Co. in Chicago pays college tuition for children of long-term employees.

5 And, at Open Market, a Boston consulting firm, employees can bring their dogs to work.

6 What's going on here? Don't these companies know that the rest of the corporate world has, seemingly, declared war on employees?

7 Why are they being so nice?

8 Despite extensive downsizing at many companies—and the feeling of alienation among remaining employees—the "most progressive companies today don't stop at focusing on profit; they're also focusing on the profit-makers: the employees."

9 So says Jim Harris of Indian Rocks Beach, Fla., a management consultant who specializes in "high performance management" and is president of the firm that bears his name.

10 Harris, whose client base includes Fortune 500 companies, also is the author of "Getting Employees to Fall in Love With Your Company" (AMACOM,

$17.95), a book that surprises in today's anorexic job market because it encourages employers to be kind to employees if they want to retain them.

11 "America's No. 1 business problem is not generating profit, because we have become brilliant at squeezing pennies to the bottom line," said Harris, who has a doctorate in speech communications from the University of Florida. "The problem today is how to maintain a loyal, committed work force. Companies that have the attitude that employees don't matter are losing their best workers."

12 The solution is for employers to capture workers' hearts, Harris says. "Excellence isn't possible with a disengaged heart. If employers don't do that, they are merely creating an environment of warm bodies."

13 Harris knows labor market realities. "My career is typical," he said. "In the 1980s, I was outplaced, downsized and fired from three major U.S. corporations. All three were the result of corporate reorganization. I understand the tenuous relationship that exists between employees and management."

14 Harris counsels his corporate clients not to forget that "the only competitive advantage in the next decade isn't marketing or technology—anybody can buy those. The real edge is the quality of your work force: Can you retain the best and the brightest?"

15 Though cynical observers might point out to Harris that urging companies to use positive rein-

forcement to motivate their employees might be like installing wall-to-wall carpeting on the Titanic, Harris says employees will respond.

16 He also says he has a data base of hundreds of examples of companies trying to establish a happy workplace, among them the "most successful and profitable companies," such as Southwest Airlines, which calls its human resource department the "People Department"; Home Depot Inc.; Ben & Jerry's Homemade Inc.; and North American Tool & Dye Co.

17 "Loyalty isn't dead," said Harris, referring to employers and workers. "It's just being re-defined."

18 The Society for Human Resource Management, based in Alexandria, Va., also sees the value of happy employees. "Innovative employee benefits incorporate changing lifestyles and allow companies to attract and retain talented employees," it concludes in its survey of 308 association members.

19 Family-friendly benefits are the way to achieve employee satisfaction, the society says. Fifty percent of the firms offer flex time; 24 percent, job sharing; 23 percent, compressed work weeks; and 20 percent child care referral and telecommuting.

20 But telecommuting may be a problem: If you work from home, can you bring your dog to the office?

21 Send e-mail to ckleiman@tribune.com.

Postreading

I. Getting the Message

After reading the article, indicate if each statement is true (T) or false (F).

1. _____ This article is mainly about how companies in the United States treat their employees badly.

2. _____ According to Jim Harris, some successful companies know that employee satisfaction is important.

3. _____ Jim Harris thinks the biggest problem facing corporations today is finding ways to increase profits.

4. _____ According to the article, most employees today feel great loyalty toward their employers.

5. _____ Jim Harris knows from personal experience what it feels like to be fired from a job.

6. _____ Keeping good employees is a problem for many companies.

7. _____ Some companies offer attractive benefits to employees' families.

8. _____ According to the article, doing laundry at work and bringing pets to work are examples of benefits that increase employee satisfaction.

Check your answers with the key on page 165. If you have made mistakes, reread the article to gain a better understanding of it.

II. Expanding Your Vocabulary

Getting Meaning from Context

Find each word below in the paragraph indicated in parentheses. Use context clues to determine the meaning of the word. Choose the best definition.

1. extensive (8)   a. large in amount   b. outside the company
2. alienation (8)   a. loyalty   b. lack of connection or affection
3. progressive (8)   a. traditional   b. advancing
4. anorexic (10)   a. modern, new   b. thin, unhealthy
5. retain (10)   a. help   b. keep
6. tenuous (13)   a. not strong   b. happy
7. cynical (15)   a. negative   b. positive
8. motivate (15)   a. discourage   b. encourage
9. innovative (18)   a. new and creative   b. profit-making

Postreading

III. Working with Idioms and Expressions

Study the meanings of the idioms and expressions below. A form of each one appears in the paragraph indicated in parentheses.

get something done (1) do or finish something

on the premises (1) at the place itself

What's going on? (6) What is happening?

bear a name (9) have the same name as someone

squeeze pennies (11) be very careful about expenses

fall in love (10) experience a strong feeling of fondness for someone or something

capture someone's heart (12) win someone's affection

the best and the brightest (14) the finest people available

see the value of something (18) appreciate or value something

telecommuting (19) working for a business at home by using telephones, computers, and other technology

Now answer the questions below with *yes* or *no*. Pay particular attention to the meanings of the idioms and expressions in *italic* print.

1. If a boss *sees the value of an employee*, does the boss probably want the employee to stay at the company? _____
2. When employees *fall in love* with the company, do they want to quit and get new jobs? _____
3. Do people who *squeeze pennies* go over the limit on their credit cards? _____
4. Does Ameritech, the communications corporation, *bear the name* of the inventor of the telephone, Alexander Graham Bell? _____

IV. Making Sense of Sentences

Find each phrase below in the paragraph indicated in parentheses. Use context clues to determine the meaning of the phrase. Then choose the statement that best expresses the meaning.

1. declared war on employees (6)
   a. treated employees like soldiers
   b. acted hostile toward employees
2. focusing on profit (8)
   a. working only to make money
   b. studying economics
3. employees don't matter (11)
   a. employees don't have feelings
   b. employees aren't important to the goals of a company

4. warm bodies (12)
   a. people excited about their work
   b. people uninterested in their work
5. the real edge (14)
   a. the actual advantage
   b. the true limit
6. employees will respond (15)
   a. workers will do better work
   b. workers will fail

Postreading

V. Talking and Writing

Discuss the topics below. Then choose one of them to write about.

1. Do you think American companies generally are treating employees better? Based on your own working experience and the daily news reports on TV and in the newspaper, do you think the atmosphere at work is improving for people?

2. In the American business world today, most employees work for several different employers in the course of their working careers. Is this true in your native country? Why or why not?

3. The article mentions job benefits such as paying college tuition for children of employees, allowing employees to do laundry at work, and providing child care referral. Can you think of other policies that would make a workplace more employee-friendly? If you have a job, what benefits would improve your own workplace?

4. Some companies are criticized for offering cheap benefits instead of higher salary. Do you think benefits like "water fights at the end of major projects" provide better encouragement to employees than more money?

Focus on Culture

Chicago Tribune

Setting the Scene

Business is what drives U.S. *consumer culture.* In this kind of society, much of life is directed toward *consumption,* or buying goods and services. Business not only provides those goods and services, but it also provides the jobs necessary to keep the consumer culture going.

In the United States people turn to their newspapers for business news that affects their lives directly or indirectly. This news is found mainly in the business section, but it can also be found almost anywhere in the newspaper. For example, a paper might print an editorial that discusses the policies of the Federal Reserve Bank or a rate increase by a utility company.

Here are a few of the kinds of business articles that a newspaper might contain:
- Feature stories or profiles of general interest about business executives
- News stories about advances or setbacks in particular corporations
- Feature stories of broad interest about new products or technology developed or being developed by corporations
- News stories about rising and falling stock prices, interest rates, unemployment rates, and retail sales
- Opinion columns about general trends in the business world and economy
- News stories about disputes between labor and management

Exercise 1. Reading Headlines: Who's ahead? Who's behind?

The United States is a very competitive society, and the business section of the newspaper, like the sports section, is partly a record of winners and losers. Business is based on competition, so readers are always curious about profit and loss, growth and decline, weakness and strength.

Here are some terms often used in newspaper headlines about business:

auto manufacturers	telephone companies	inflation
downsizing	housing	recession
stocks	GNP	unemployment
CEO	nonprofit organizations	foreign investment
Japanese industries	interest rate	retail
advertising	consumer demand	labor unions
debt	public relations	Internet

Chicago Tribune

Focus on Culture

Look through the business section of your local newspaper and find headlines that use some of the terms on page 30. Then check whether the article is about a positive development—*Getting Ahead*—or a negative development—*Falling Behind*.

	Term	Headline	Getting Ahead	Falling Behind
1.				
2.				
3.				
4.				
5.				
6.				
7.				
8.				

Exercise 2. Analyzing a Business Article

Choose one of the articles from those above and answer these questions about it.

1. What is the headline? Is the headline difficult to understand? How does it help you predict the content of the article?
2. Who wrote the article? How is the author identified? For example, the author could be a staff writer (a writer employed by the paper), an expert economist, a columnist, or a reporter from another newspaper whose column is being reprinted.
3. What is the purpose of the article? Is it to give a factual report, record expert opinions on an economic issue, argue the opinion of the author, give financial advice, or something else?
4. Write down three new vocabulary terms that give you difficulty. Write their definitions and try to use each in a sentence.
5. Is the article one that could appear in a newspaper in your native country or not? Explain.

Chicago Tribune

Focus on Culture

Exercise 3. How's Business?

Scan the newspaper business section for a few weeks and look for information about general business conditions in your area. As you read, look for answers to the questions below. Be prepared to discuss your conclusions with the class.

1. Is it difficult to find a job right now? Why or why not? In what fields are employment opportunities best?
2. What are some good investment opportunities now, according to the experts?
3. What economic problems does your area face at this time?
4. What is the overall economic outlook—optimistic or pessimistic?

Exercise 4. Comparing Business Stories

Find an important, widely covered national business story, one that has also been covered on television news. Examples might include a dispute between labor and management, a projected downsizing in a big corporation, or a technological innovation that could change the telecommunications industry. Read a story about the issue in your local newspaper. Then go to the library and read an article from some other newspaper on the same topic. Note the similarities and differences.

1. Which article gives more basic information about the issue?
2. Do both articles emphasize the same aspects of the issue? How does the focus of one differ from the focus of the other?
3. Does one article seem more objective than the other? How?
4. Which article did you enjoy more? Why?

Exercise 5. Journal Assignment: It's Your Business

Over a two-week period, find three business stories that you think will affect your life in some way. Are there layoffs at a local plant? Are there new jobs in the computer industry? Is there a rise in meat prices? Is there a problem with access to the Internet? For each article write down the headline, briefly summarize the story, and tell how the issue might affect your own life.

Chicago Tribune

SectionThree
Lifestyles

1
Tales in English give fresh voice to foreign lands

2
The delights of downsizing

3
New Year's wish list runs from fitness to forests

Focus on Culture

Lifestyles

Chicago Tribune

Lifestyles

Choosing the Way We Live

Are you single or married? Are you a cat owner or a dog owner? Do you exercise, or are you a "couch potato"? Do you live in a house or an apartment? These questions, and many others—some much more serious than others—are about your lifestyle.

People in the United States feel that they can choose their lifestyles and even shape their own identities. In other societies this is not necessarily true. For example, in many countries people's attitudes, tastes, moral standards, and habits closely correspond to those of their social class, determined more or less at birth. But the individualism and personal freedom of the United States mean that immigrants not only can make a new world for themselves but can also choose a new way of life.

The great variety of lifestyles in the United States leads to constant national discussion of the choices that people make. This freedom of choice is fun and exciting, but it also creates stress and uncertainty. In newspapers lifestyle issues are discussed in the features or style section. In the *Chicago Tribune* this section is called "Tempo." People turn to this section for lively discussion of the lifestyle choices they face with regard to their personal identities, their families, and their social lives.

Many people believe that they can make their lives happy and satisfying despite their problems. If they lack confidence or tend to feel anxious, shy, angry, or depressed, they believe that they can change themselves. *Self-help* books, magazines, and feature articles are filled with advice from therapists and experts about steps to take to become a more happy or fulfilled person and to raise one's *self-esteem*. Part of this search for self-improvement is a belief that even one's own appearance can be controlled. This is why there are so many articles in the newspaper about looking young, wearing the latest fashions, and becoming physically fit.

Lifestyle choices also involve moral and social issues. How should children be raised? How should people behave on a date? How should elderly people be treated? How can people stay happily married? How much time should be devoted to work and how much to family? All these kinds of issues are constantly discussed and are constantly changing. Not only are experts such as psychologists and clergy consulted, but celebrities from the political and entertainment worlds are held up as lifestyle leaders as well. In the newspaper, feature articles called *profiles* discuss in detail the personal lives or public work of movie stars, authors, community leaders, artists, and exceptional individuals who are not celebrities. The lifestyle choices these people make contribute to the public discussion of all the issues that people think about.

A well-known advertising slogan is "Just do it." In the culture of the United States, people believe that they can take action and become the kind of people they want to be and live the way they want to live.

Chicago Tribune

Preparation

Tales in English give fresh voice to foreign lands

Previewing the Article

What's *your* story? As this article shows, learners of English have fascinating stories to tell about leaving their native countries and facing a new life. When an enterprising college teacher asked his students to tell their stories and later collected them in a book, the writers discovered that they had crossed the biggest cultural barrier of all—language. From being on the outside of a new culture, they had taken a step inside. What had once seemed too personal and difficult to tell now seemed like a bridge to a new world of English speakers.

This class is typical of many college classes in the Chicago area, which has at least a hundred different ethnic groups and a growing immigrant population. English-as-a-Second Language classes have become common at nearly every college and university. And such stories as these students have to tell are also of interest to newspaper readers born in the United States. Many of these readers are themselves descended from European immigrants who came to the country at the turn of the century.

This article is an example of a newspaper *column,* and the writer of the article is a *columnist.* Columnists write one or more short essays of opinion in a newspaper each week. Readers grow to like particular columnists and look forward to reading them on the days when their work appears. Columnists help to make a newspaper more personal and to increase reader loyalty.

Before You Read

Discuss these questions:
1. Have you ever told your story about leaving your native country and coming to the United States? Would you feel comfortable about publishing it in a book? Could you read it to a public audience?
2. On U.S. daytime television there are many talk shows in which people tell very personal stories about their lives. Would people from your native country feel comfortable about doing this?
3. As your ability to speak English grows, do you feel that you are becoming more of an "insider" in American life? Has there ever been a particular event or conversation that made you feel this way?

As You Read

Look for answers to the following questions:
1. Why did the teacher collect the students' stories in a book?
2. Does the author think the teacher should have made more corrections in the students' stories as they appear in the book?
3. What can people who aren't immigrants learn by reading these stories?

TALES IN
English
give fresh voice to foreign lands

Mary Schmich

1   All of us carry around inside us the story of our lives, a covert world of all the things we've thought and seen and done. Our experiences, which survive so vividly inside us, are held hostage in our hearts, locked away from public view.

2   But if we're lucky, every now and then we find the right words and an audience, and we get the chance to pull a piece of the story from the vault and show it off. We make what's lost come alive again.

3   Michael McColly's students have gotten lucky.

4   "I was like blind and mute because I was unable to read, to write, to speak or to understand the language of where I was living."

5   —Margarita Espinoza, an immigrant from Mexico, on her early days in Chicago.

6   With his gilded, tousled hair, McColly at 39 looks more like an L.A. surfer than what he is—professor McColly of Northeastern Illinois University, teacher of English as a Second Language. For 4 years he has done what the legions of such teachers do, given sight and speech to immigrants like Margarita Espinoza by teaching them to parse and spell.

7   But McColly has gone a step further.

8   With a $750 grant and an editing pencil, he has compiled his students' stories into a book called "The World is Round: Narratives of ESL Students."

9   These are seemingly ordinary Chicagoans telling stories that will grab your heart and stomp on it. They are stories of escape—from Vietnam by boat, from Eritrea by camel, from Mexico in a car trunk. They are stories of arriving in the promised land—the land of cockroaches and greasy stoves, of thin mattresses tossed on floors, of luxuries like the bathroom door that shuts. They are stories of parents who drive cabs and clean restrooms in the hopes of giving their children something better.

10 The book is a humble creation, and McColly apologizes for the simple cardboard cover. "It's the stories," he says, "that count."

11 "In my country if you got married with someone older than you by five or more years, people behind your back will laugh at you. Like me, when I went to school my friends at school laughed at me. Many times my tears almost came out, but I tried to keep them in my eyes."

12 —Loan Le, a Vietnamese refugee, recounting her forced betrothal at age 14 to a man 10 years older.

13 The essays in "The World is Round" started out as McColly's assignments to his classes: Write about a place from your past. Write about someone you know. Write about arriving in America.

14 What emerged was a world hidden from most Chicagoans, a world that falls to younger immigrants to convey since many of their parents never learn English.

15 "I didn't have any friends because I was just a newcomer, and I couldn't speak English; therefore, I always stayed home and watched TV. Sometimes, I wanted to take a walk, but I was afraid to get lost."

16 —Bryan Phung, a Vietnamese refugee, on his introduction to Chicago.

17 McColly was inspired to assemble the book after several of his students read their essays aloud one night at the Hot House nightclub in Wicker Park. The students cried. The audience cried.

18 These simple stories, he realized, documented experiences that went barely noticed in the mainstream media. And the students in telling them were transformed, not just by the telling but by telling their tales in English. In that moment, they felt inaugurated into an exclusive club of English speakers. Finally, they belonged.

19 Editing the essays, McColly resisted the impulse to prune the language to perfection. He saw that English in a novice's hands takes on novel hues and shapes. A peculiar poetry lies in what we would call mistakes.

20 "Then it was finally time to go. . . . My dad took my hand and squeezed really hard. Then he gave me a hug. I whispered in his ear, 'I'm never coming back here.' As he looked at me in the eyes, a tear smuggled down his cheek, and he simply said, 'I know.'"

21 —Josip Marich, a Bosnian refugee on fleeing the war in his homeland.

22 Stories, it has been said, are a way of keeping the past present. This modest little book gives us a glimpse of the past that the immigrants in this city carry in them, lets us peek into distant places where America means the dream of freedom and a Walkman, lets us travel to foreign worlds where tears smuggle down a cheek.

23 E-mail: mtschmich@aol.com

Postreading

I. Getting the Message

After you read the article, choose the best answer for each item.

1. The main idea of this article is that
   a. immigrant students felt better about their lives in America after telling their stories in English.
   b. the student writers had not yet learned to write proper English.
   c. students sometimes risk their lives to come to the United States.

2. The author believes that Michael McColly looks
   a. like a typical college professor.
   b. handsome and young for his age.
   c. serious and middle-aged.

3. The author says that
   a. immigrants have the best stories.
   b. everyone has a story to tell.
   c. only a few people can tell a good story.

4. The stories in the book
   a. began as normal writing assignments in an ESL class.
   b. were all corrected and rewritten by the teacher.
   c. have become famous all over the country.

5. The book is valuable to readers because
   a. it helps readers understand immigrants.
   b. it tells about the politics of other countries.
   c. it informs readers about important world issues.

Check your answers with the key on page 165. If you have made mistakes, reread the article to gain a better understanding of it.

II. Expanding Your Vocabulary

A. Getting Meaning from Context

Find each word or phrase in the paragraph indicated in parentheses. Use context clues to determine the meaning of the word. Choose the best definition.

1. covert (1)	a. hidden	b. protected
2. legions (6)	a. groups	b. large numbers
3. compiled (8)	a. criticized	b. gathered together
4. betrothal (12)	a. kidnapping	b. engagement for marriage
5. emerged (4)	a. came out	b. started
6. inaugurated (18)	a. introduced	b. sent away
7. novice (19)	a. a beginner	b. an experienced person

B. Using Figurative Language

Each italicized word or phrase below has a literal meaning that the author uses to suggest another, figurative meaning. Find the word in the paragraph indicated in parentheses. Reread the paragraph. Then answer each question.

1. A *vault* (2) is an underground room where valuable things are stored. What then does the author mean by saying we can "pull a piece of the story from the vault"?

2. The expression *promised land* (9) originally referred to the land promised by God in the Bible to the Hebrews fleeing Egypt. What is the *promised land* referred to here?

3. To *prune* (19) a tree is to cut off branches in order to help it grow or improve its shape. What does "pruning" language mean?

Postreading

III. Working with Idioms and Expressions

Find each italicized expression in the paragraph indicated in parentheses. Reread the paragraph. Then answer the questions.

1. If a memory is *held hostage* (1), what is being done to it?
2. How do we choose part of our life story and *show it off* (2)?
3. If someone says something about you *behind your back* (11), what has the person done?
4. Why did the job of telling the story of the hidden immigrant world *fall to* (14) the younger generation?
5. Why would a newcomer to a big city be afraid to *get lost* (15)?
6. Why do you think the fascinating stories of recent immigrants *went barely noticed* (18) in the press and television?
7. Why did the father cry as he *gave a hug* (20) to his son?
8. How can a book *give a glimpse* (22) of "the past that the immigrants in this city carry in them"?
9. In what way do teachers *give sight and speech to* (6) immigrant students? Is this similar to the way a tale can "*give fresh voice to* a foreign land"? (See the headline.)
10. Numbers 7–9 above show how important the verb *give* is in English. Does the equivalent word in your own language also have a wide variety of uses? Present a few examples.

IV. Talking and Writing

Discuss the following topics. Then choose one of them to write about.

1. Before immigrants arrive in the United States, they have expectations about U.S. culture. What surprised you most about the way people live in the United States?
2. The author says that there are distant lands where "America means the dream of freedom and a Walkman." A Walkman (a Sony-brand portable radio with head-phones) is used here as a symbol. Why is it a good symbol of U.S. culture? Can you think of other products that would be good symbols of the American way of life? Could a particular manufactured product be used to symbolize your own culture? Explain.
3. Bryan Phung, one of the student writers, remembered how he "always stayed home and watched TV" when he first arrived because he was afraid to go out. Have you ever felt that way? What advice would you give a newcomer to break out of this situation?
4. What do you think is meant by the title of the book *The World is Round*? Why would this be a good name for a collection of stories by recent immigrants?

Chicago Tribune

Preparation

The delights of downsizing

Previewing the Article

Have you ever gone shopping for one thing and come home with several other things? Have you ever bought a second TV or paid extra for a pair of running shoes with a famous basketball player's name on them? Then you are a part of the *consumer culture.* In the United States people love to *consume,* or buy, a great variety of things that they do not really need: video cameras, sport vehicles, giant TV sets, designer clothes, or prepackaged frozen dinners, for example.

Some people are not happy about this, however, and they have started a movement called *Voluntary Simplicity.* These people choose to lead a simpler life that is not so dependent on material possessions. They choose to *downsize* their lives: they may leave high-paying jobs for ones with less pay, or they may sell big expensive houses and move to smaller ones. Though they learn to reduce the scale of their living, they remain financially comfortable even after down-sizing. Many other people in the United States, of course, must do this involuntarily, without choosing to do it, because of debt, unemployment, limited income, or other troubles.

The writer of this opinion essay makes fun of Voluntary Simplicity. He believes that as a parent of young children he is in no position to choose a simpler life for his family. He also makes fun of himself and shows that there is much in his family's lifestyle to laugh about.

The humor in the article is based on *irony,* that is, saying the opposite of what is meant. Thus the writer pretends that he has chosen a fashionable lifestyle when he really means that his way of living is ordinary and not fashionable at all.

Before You Read

Discuss the following questions:
1. What does the headline mean? Have you read newspaper stories about downsizing? What does it mean when a company downsizes?
2. How does the arrival of children change life for a married couple? How does it change their daily schedule and their living space for example?
3. This article is about a *lifestyle trend* called Voluntary Simplicity. Can you think of any other lifestyle trends—involving exercise, diet, work, or leisure time activities—that are popular with people you know?

As You Read

Look for examples of irony. How does the writer show the reader that he means the opposite of what he says?

The delights of downsizing

Advice for the simple life: Try parenthood

By Robert Hughes
SPECIAL TO THE TRIBUNE

1 When I first read about the lifestyle trend of the '90s called Voluntary Simplicity, I let out an involuntary chuckle that traveled right through a cackle into an involuntary guffaw.

2 "Ha!" I laughed as I read the stories about the couples who have given up their stressful high-paying jobs and "downshifted" to living the simple life on the interest from their investments, clipping coupons from the supermarket, baking their own bread and keeping up a high profile of conspicuous smugness.

3 How sad, how retro, how hopelessly out of step, for without fanfare and press releases, my wife and I find ourselves several laps ahead of this movement, having long ago passed up Voluntary Simplicity and systematically downshifted to a better and simpler way of life.

4 Stage 1: The Marriage Downshift. Before we were married, Ellen and I had every reason to believe that we had a life of luxury and ease ahead. Visiting our multiple residences throughout the year, keeping a watchful eye on our polo ponies and driving our behemoth off-the-road vehicles to ski resorts were just some of the activities we used to fantasize about while sipping strong coffee in her tiny studio apartment.

5 But realizing in advance the sheer stress and shallowness of this sort of crass consumption, we opted for a more spiritual existence by downshifting to the plane of ordinary married folk.

6 Stage 2: The Parenting Downshift. When we were first married, we looked around us at our lifestyle with its nights out at the latest films, its uninterrupted conversations, its several working household appliances, and knew there had to be less.

7 Living for ourselves and our possessions was cloying and dis-

Illustration by Danny Shanahan

honest. The simple needs and simple smiles of children were what we needed to gain perspective and prioritize our values.

8 When we look back on it, the fascinating lifestyle aspect of the decision to have children is this: It is the last voluntary thing we have ever done.

9 Stage 3: The Involuntary Downshift. Before parenthood, our two-bedroom house seemed unnecessarily opulent and vast, like Citizen Kane's Xanadu. The arrival of our two little boys, now aged 5 and 7, solved this problem brilliantly, freeing us from bourgeois reliance on open space, unbroken furniture and Lego-free carpeting.

10 Today when I walk into the home of someone with young children and my host feels no need to warn me about the chair I'm about to sit on, I know I'm in the house of someone who badly needs a good downshifting.

11 The beauty of this stage is that you feel like you've moved to a smaller house without actually buying one. Each room seems about half its original size, and all this happened without having to deal with real estate agents.

12 Stage 4: The Undersizing Downshift. The big problem with the Voluntary Simplicity move-

ment is that it doesn't go far enough—the rich downshift to just the right point to fulfill basic needs. True simplicity, however, means going past that point.

13 For instance, they never seem to drive truly downsized cars. I do. Our sometimes reliable 1988 Escort, like-new in that about 30 percent of its working parts have been replaced, takes a certain amount of social courage to drive.

14 When my sons say things like, "Why do we drive such a stupid car, Dad?" I smile and reply that they will understand when they grow up. For the truth is, when I look up at the gleaming mini-vans that pass us on the highway, I'm proud to know I'm in the company of Gandhi, St. Francis, Buddha and other non-materialist giants of history.

15 Stage 5: Absolute Simplicity. Formerly wealthy downshifters always note that they now have more time for things that really matter to them, like long walks at sunset, discussing books with friends and preparing elaborate meals from vegetables grown in their own gardens.

16 Read a book? Grow a vegetable? Take a walk? The child-downshifted household eliminates all these confusing choices that cause stress in modern life.

17 These days, for example, my wife and I can relax in the knowledge that every evening for the foreseeable future will be spent doing homework. We will sit patiently through hour after hour of quality time, enriching our children with our extensive knowledge of 2nd, 3rd, and 4th grade math, modeling for them the advice of Henry David Thoreau to "simplify, simplify, simplify."

18 The downwardly mobile aristocracy has a lot to learn from us, the absolutely simple folks. They should watch us carefully for the next lifestyle trend. From what I hear about raising teenagers, we just might push through the outside of the envelope and into Total Complexity.

19 Stay tuned.

Chicago Tribune

Postreading

I. Getting the Message

After reading the article, choose the best answer for each item.

1. The writer says that he laughs when he reads stories about the new lifestyle trend because
   a. he is already living a simple life.
   b. the Voluntary Simplicity movement can teach him a lot.
   c. he doesn't want to live a simple life.

2. Before marriage he and his wife probably
   a. were not rich.
   b. owned many expensive things.
   c. planned to start a lifestyle trend.

3. The writer and his wife
   a. have two children.
   b. have three children.
   c. have four children.

4. The writer and his wife live in
   a. a small apartment.
   b. a very large house.
   c. a house with two bedrooms.

5. The writer's children
   a. enjoy riding in the family car.
   b. dislike the family car.
   c. agree with their father about the family car.

Check your answers with the key on page 165. If you have made mistakes, reread the article to gain a better understanding of it.

II. Expanding Your Vocabulary

A. Getting Meaning from Context

Find each word in the paragraph indicated in parentheses. Then choose the best definition.

1. trend (1)   a. moral teaching   b. current style, fashion
2. systematically (3)   a. quickly   b. in an organized way
3. luxury (4)   a. wealth and comfort   b. energy
4. opted (5)   a. wished   b. chose
5. prioritize (7)   a. arrange according   b. make limits
                               to importance
6. opulent (9)   a. rich, plentiful   b. empty
7. elaborate (15)   a. simple   b. complicated
8. eliminates (16)   a. helps   b. gets rid of
9. foreseeable (17)   a. able to be forced   b. predictable

B. Working with Synonyms

Chuckle, cackle, and *guffaw* (paragraph 1) all mean "laugh." But each word has a slightly different meaning. Based on the context of paragraph 1, match the word on the left with its meaning on the right.

1. _____ chuckle   a. an extremely loud burst of laughter
2. _____ cackle   b. a high, sharp, unpleasant laugh
3. _____ guffaw   c. a quiet laugh

Chicago Tribune

Postreading

III. Working with Idioms and Expressions

Study the meanings of the following idioms and expressions:

downsize (headline) 1. to lay off workers in order to function more efficiently or
reduce costs 2. to reduce the size of something

let out (1) express

downshift (2) live at a slower pace, like a car shifting into a lower gear

conspicuous smugness (2) a play on words: the real expression is *conspicuous consumption.* This refers to people buying expensive things in order to appear wealthy.

clip coupons (2) cut ads out of the newspaper that grant discounts on store items

the simple life (2) an ideal way of life that is not dependent on having material
possessions

keep up a high profile (2) appearing to be rich and upper class

retro (3) old-fashioned

out of step (3) not fashionable

keep a watchful eye on (4) take great care of

downwardly mobile (18) a play on words: people in the United States consider themselves *upwardly mobile,* that is, they move from a lower standard of living to a
higher one.

Complete the sentences below with the idioms and expressions above.

1. People trying to save money at the supermarket often _____ to save money.

2. When companies _____ , many workers have a difficult time finding other jobs.

3. When people buy extremely expensive cars and worry about them being stolen, they need to

   _____ them.

4. For many people, living _____ is just a dream because they lead complicated lives.

IV. Focusing on Style and Tone

To create a humorous tone, this article uses much *verbal irony.* When people use verbal irony, they say one thing but *imply*, or mean without stating directly, the opposite.
For example, if a person says in the middle of a big rainstorm, "Boy, this sure is a
beautiful day," the speaker implies that the weather is terrible. The writer of this article
pretends to think that he has cleverly chosen a superior way of life but implies that
he has not really done so.

Chicago Tribune

Postreading

In this exercise read the brief quotation from the article and then choose the answer that reflects the implied meaning. The first one has been done for you.

1. "the simple needs and simple smiles of children" (7)
   - (a.) Children's needs are not simple.
   - b. Children are easy for parents to raise.
2. "Our two-bedroom house seemed unnecessarily opulent and vast." (9)
   - a. The house seemed very big.
   - b. The house seemed small.
3. "The beauty of this stage is that you feel like you've moved to a smaller house without actually buying one." (11)
   - a. He likes his small house and doesn't want a bigger one.
   - b. He would like to have a bigger house.
4. "our sometimes reliable 1988 Escort, like-new in that about 30 percent of its working parts have been replaced . . ." (13)
   - a. The car runs well and is almost new.
   - b. The car seldom runs well.
5. "when I look up at the gleaming mini-vans that pass us on the highway, I'm proud to know I'm in the company of Gandhi, St. Francis, Buddha and other non-materialist giants of history." (14)
   - a. He is embarrassed to be driving his car.
   - b. His car makes him feel like a spiritual person.
6. "The downwardly mobile aristocracy has a lot to learn from us, the absolutely simple folks." (18)
   - a. The writer's lifestyle should be imitated.
   - b. The writer's lifestyle should not be imitated.

V. Talking and Writing

Discuss the topics below. Then choose one of them to write about.

1. Compare attitudes toward shopping in the United States and in your native country. Do the Americans you know seem too interested in shopping? Is shopping a common topic of conversation in your native country?
2. When people live on a budget, they carefully limit how much they spend and avoid using credit cards. Is it more difficult to live on a budget in the United States than in your native country? Why or why not?
3. Is Voluntary Simplicity, or something like it, a lifestyle trend in your own native country? Explain.
4. Like this author, U.S. comedians on television often laugh at themselves and the way they live. Do you do this? Do you enjoy U.S. television comedians? How important is laughter for relieving stress?

Chicago Tribune

Preparation

New Year's wish list runs from fitness to forests

Previewing the Article

Every New Year we promise ourselves the same things: *this* year we will stop smoking, or lose ten pounds, or eat more vegetables, or be nicer to our mother-in-law. And every year we get the same mixed results: we start out doing pretty well, and then, more often than not, we slowly slip back into our old ways of living.

As this article vividly shows, these little promises, called "New Year's resolutions," are very popular in the United States. People are ever hopeful about self-improvement, and because of their belief in a free individual's power to start over and create a new identity in a new world, they earnestly try each year to do better.

One very visible result of this urge to reshape one-self is the exercise class. As the writer of the article points out, people in the United States today turn to exercise as a way to begin a new year with a fresh attitude. Classes like these, along with support groups and the many *self-help* books that are published every year, all help people to overcome personal obstacles such as bad habits or low self-esteem.

The article is based on interviews with people in Arlington Heights, a suburb of Chicago with a population of 66,116 people.

Before You Read

Discuss the following questions:
1. Did you make a New Year's resolution this past year? What was it? Were you successful in achieving it?
2. In the headline for this article, what does the word *runs* mean? Look up *run* in a college dictionary. How many definitions are there? Why are there so many? Is there an equivalent word for *run* in your own language?

As You Read

Count the number of separate New Year's resolutions that are mentioned in the article. Do you think that these are a good sample of the kinds of resolutions that people make? Can you think of other typical resolutions?

wish list

runs from fitness to forests

Dimitra DeFotis

1 To hear Rick Poole tell it, the only sure way to turn one's New Year's resolutions into reality is to weave them into everyday life, not just January.

2 And he should know. As athletic supervisor for the Arlington Heights Park District, Poole watches the rosters of aerobics, fitness and basketball sessions swell with the beginning of each new year, only to drop off by as much as a third by summer.

3 An athletic sort since he was a child, Poole does not make resolutions.

4 "I'm a lifestyle change person, not a resolution person," he said. "I just think that a change should be a gradual lifestyle change, not a sudden change."

5 A sampling of Arlington Heights leaders and average citizens shows most people wish for achievable goals, whether for their personal lives or the world.

6 When asked his resolution for 1997, Derek Nelson, a 10-year-old pupil at Stitt School, thought carefully.

7 Top on his list is saving rain forests.

8 "We're studying that now because they are endangered," Derek said. "More and more are being cut every day, and the forests are many animals' homes."

9 And his second resolution?

10 "Well, probably to not talk as much in school," he said.

Aerobics instructor Marilyn Duda leads a class at the Arlington Heights Park District. Participation in fitness activities usually swells at the start of each year, park officials say, but falls off by summer.
Tribune photo by Val Mazzenga.

11 Village President Arlene Mulder, a former physical education teacher and girls basketball coach, said she wants extra hours in the day to exercise, a stable U.S. economy and world peace, and to win her mayoral re-election bid—not necessarily in that order.

12 If there is a cynic in town, it is Antonio Riesco. The co-owner of La Tasca tapas restaurant in downtown Arlington Heights said he just wants to be around long enough to lift a toast to 1998.

13 "I always make it the same resolution, to make it to the next year," said the Arlington Heights resident.

14 As for the rest of the world? Does he want world peace or to save the rain forests?

15 "For the world, I could care less," Riesco said. "If I'm not here making contributions, who cares? That sounds selfish, but that's life."

16 Ed Searing, principal of Riley Elementary School, casts a broader net. He wants to get the school hooked to the Internet so that children can expand their learning. "First children learn about friends and family, then community, then Chicago, Illinois and the world," Searing said. "What better way to learn that than to get on the Internet and experience it?"

Chicago Tribune
Postreading

I. Getting the Message

After reading the article, indicate if each statement is true (T) or false (F). For help, check the paragraph number indicated in parentheses.

1. _____ The example of the park district program shows that new year's resolutions about fitness are usually very effective. (2)
2. _____ Most of the people the reporter talked to wished for realistic goals. (5)
3. _____ The article is the result of a scientific survey of thousands of Arlington Heights residents. (5)
4. _____ The president of Arlington Heights is a restaurant owner. (11)
5. _____ Antonio Riesco resolves to become more physically fit every year. (13)

Check your answers with the key on page 165. If you have made any mistakes, reread the article to gain a better understanding of it.

II. Expanding Your Vocabulary

Getting Meaning from Context

Find each word in the paragraph indicated in parentheses. Use context clues to determine the meaning of the word. Choose the best definition.

1. achievable (5)   a. desirable   b. can be done
2. endangered (8)   a. nearly gone   b. creating danger
3. stable (11)   a. unchanging   b. large
4. cynic (12)   a. negative person   b. happy person
5. contributions (15) a. comments   b. helpful acts
6. expand (16)   a. make bigger   b. start

Postreading

III. Working with Idioms and Expressions

Find each phrase in the paragraph indicated in parentheses. Choose the answer that best conveys the meaning of the phrase.

1. When Rick Poole says the best way to turn "resolutions into reality" is "to weave them into everyday life" (1), he means that
   a. people need to be stronger and make more resolutions.
   b. people need to make changes a part of daily living.
2. That the number of people in fitness classes *"swells"* in January "only to drop off by as much as a third" by summer (2) implies that
   a. people have trouble keeping their New Year's resolutions.
   b. people have trouble making New Year's resolutions.
3. When Antonio Riesco says he "just wants to be around" (12) until 1998 and that he wants "to make it to" (13) the next year, he means that
   a. he simply wants to stay alive another year.
   b. he wants to make money and be prosperous for another year.
4. When Antonio Riesco says, "I could care less" (15), he means that
   a. he doesn't care.
   b. he cares very much.
5. "Casts a broader net" (16) means
   a. that the principal wants to accomplish more.
   b. that the principal does not believe he can do very much.

IV. Talking and Writing

Discuss the topics below. Then choose one of them to write about.

1. Typical New Year's resolutions in the United States are related to personal improvement: getting physically fit, losing weight, eating a healthier diet, reading more books, spending more time with one's children. Would these and other resolutions mentioned in the article be typical in your native country? Why or why not?
2. If you were to make a New Year's resolution right now, what would it be? What steps would be necessary to achieve this goal?

Chicago Tribune

Focus on Culture

Setting the Scene

In many ways, articles in the features or lifestyle section present a newspaper's most direct look at the culture of the United States. In this section writers discuss people's habits, attitudes, customs, and moral standards in the most direct way. For example, a feature story might tell readers about strategies for getting children to read books instead of watching television. Or a profile might tell the inspirational life story of a disabled person who became a community leader. Such topics are not only entertaining but reveal much about how people live. Lifestyle issues are discussed in features, news stories, profiles, advice columns, regular columns of opinion by newspaper staff, "how-to" articles, essays by guest columnists, health-care reports, and even comics.

Exercise 1. Finding Lifestyle Issues in the Newspaper

In this exercise scan the feature section of your local newspaper for a few days, find an article on each general topic below, and write (1) the title of the article, (2) the group that the article seems intended to appeal to (such as teenagers, mothers, working women, or all adult readers), (3) whether or not you liked the article, and (4) whether or not you would expect to see this kind of article in a newspaper in your native country.

	Topic	Headline	Group	Did You Like It?	Newspaper in Native Country
1.	fashion				
2.	celebrities				
3.	dating				
4.	fitness				
5.	education				
6.	child-rearing				
7.	health				
8.	elderly				
9.	psychology				

Focus on Culture

Exercise 2. Culture and Lifestyles

Imagine that you are an editor of the feature section of a newspaper. Think of three lifestyle topics that would be of particular interest to recent immigrants from your native country. In one or two sentences, explain why the topic would be interesting.

	Topic	Reason for Interest
1.		
2.		
3.		

Exercise 3. What's in a Profile?

Profiles typically are either about celebrities—such as actors, community leaders, artists, and authors—or about ordinary people with special accomplishments or experiences. Most profiles do the following:

- tell something about a person's life
- tell about the person's current work
- reveal the person's professional goals, lifestyle, family life, and attitudes toward his or her work

Find a profile in the newspaper and analyze it by answering the following questions:

1. Why did the newspaper run a profile on this person at this time?
2. Did you know anything about the person before you read the article? If so, did the article cause you to change your attitude toward this person? Did you find out anything new?
3. What aspects of the person's lifestyle are revealed in the article?
4. How does the author of the profile seem to feel toward the subject?
5. Did the article stimulate your interest in the person's work? Why or why not?
6. Would such a profile about this sort of person appear in a newspaper in your native country? Why or why not?

Chicago Tribune

Focus on Culture

Exercise 4. A New Movie Star: You

Using the style of a celebrity profile that you have read, write about yourself. In this assignment, pretend that you are a movie star being interviewed by a reporter. In addition to talking about the work you do, give truthful answers to questions such as these: What's your favorite TV show? What kind of car do you drive? Are you married? Do you have any children? What kind of home do you have? Do you belong to a church? What valuable advice did your parents give you about life? What advice would you give your children? Who are your personal heroes?

Exercise 5. Journal Assignment: What's So Funny?

Comic strips present an excellent window on culture. The comic strips in the *Chicago Tribune,* for example, reveal a great deal about particular groups: "Cathy" deals with the problems of single women; "Dilbert" portrays the frustrations of office workers; "The Buckets" portrays the difficulties of raising spirited young children; "The Lockhorns" depicts the disagreements of a married couple. In just a few words and pictures, such strips reveal how people in the United States view the problems they face in daily life.

However, comic strips present several problems to learners of English. One is their particular style of humor. Some things seem funny to people in one culture but not to people in another. Another problem is vocabulary. Comic strips often contain slang, idioms, and references to television, film, and the news—all of which may present a challenge.

Over a one-week period, find one comic strip each day that you thought was funny and answer these questions about it.

1. What is the name of the strip?
2. What group of people is the strip about?
3. Are there any new words that you need to look up in a dictionary? What are they?
4. Why is this strip funny to you?
5. Do you think this is funny only within the culture of the United States, or is the humor universal? Explain your answer.

Chicago Tribune

Focus on Culture

Sports

Sports

Breaking Barriers Through Sports

A common sight for Chicago basketball fans is this: Michael Jordan of the Bulls jumps to make a shot and then seems to pause in the air, turn, and—impossibly—rise even higher to put the ball in the basket. The amazed fans at home and in the stadium—rich and poor, white and black, foreign-born and native-born—cheer, laugh, or shake their heads. All are united in one pleasurable feeling: pride. For a few moments living in Chicago feels like living in a big family.

Sports are a great force for unity in the United States and, of course, throughout the world. In large cities like Chicago, where there is sweeping ethnic diversity along with enormous differences in class and educational background, the local sports teams pull people together and make them feel like a close community. The same is true nationally, for network and cable coverage of football, baseball, and basketball makes the teams and players seem like an everyday part of life. And on a global scale, soccer matches and the Olympic games briefly unite countries in a peaceful competition in which everyone agrees on the rules and standards of excellence.

Though love of sports is basically the same regardless of culture, two factors that color U.S. sports in a special way are money and individualism. Playing professional sports in the United States is big business. Thus, along with endless discussions of games and strategy, people in the United States are also accustomed to talking about how much money a star player makes a year, how much a new stadium will cost, or how much an advertiser will pay for 30 seconds of commercial time on a Super Bowl television broadcast.

The other factor is individualism. People in the United States love the story of the determined individual who rises from a deprived background to become a sports legend. When this happens, democracy seems to be working as it should, for sports are a democratic arena where discrimination is not supposed to play a part and where achievement isn't dependent on race, birth, or social class. Most recently, for example, Tiger Woods broke through a historic racial barrier in golf. Indeed, in sports people find an area of life where barriers of race and class are broken long before they are broken in daily life.

Of course, in the United States sports are more than entertainment, for they are woven into the fabric of daily life. College and high school sports are followed with great interest, and amateur sports of every sort are popular: an office softball team helps create team spirit in the workplace; a Saturday-morning soccer league teaches eight-year-old children the basics of playing together; a volleyball match in the evening at a sports club helps people relax after work. In every case, sports bring people together in a world where people are often driven apart.

Chicago Tribune

Preparation

Triumphant return to Titletown
Nothing cheesy about Green Bay

Previewing the Articles

In the United States every year, many people watch a football game called the Super Bowl. The 1997 match, Super Bowl XXXI, between the New England Patriots and the Green Bay Packers, was watched by 129 million people of all ages and from widely divergent cultural, class, and educational backgrounds.

The first article describes the giant celebration held in Green Bay, Wisconsin—a town with a population of 97,000—when the town's winning team, the Packers, returned from the Super Bowl. Since Green Bay is the smallest city in the United States to have an important football team, the Packers are among the town's proudest possessions. Thousands of fans came out to greet the parade of buses, or *motorcade,* to the home stadium, Lambeau Field, where a victory celebration was held.

The team's victory meant the return of the Lombardi Trophy to Green Bay. The Super Bowl award is named after Vince Lombardi (1913–1970), who coached the Packers from 1959 to 1967, but the Packers had not won the title since 1968. This is why one of the players says to the crowd, "Vince, I know you're listening. Your trophy is safe once again."

The amused tone of this article—written by a big-city reporter—reflects the difference between urban and rural attitudes. Chicago Bears fans often make jokes about Wisconsin "cheeseheads" and beer drinkers because Wisconsin is famous for its dairy and beer industries. And much of the media coverage of the Wisconsin fans reflects an urban dweller's perceptions of country people.

The article immediately following tries to correct this media-created misconception about people who are not from big cities. It is a letter to the editor from a Wisconsin reader who points out that city people are not the only ones with some education and sophistication.

Before You Read

Discuss the following questions:
1. Do you enjoy American football? Do you understand how it is played? Here are football terms used in the first article: *defensive coordinator, linebacker, lineman, defensive end, tight end, kickoff, touchdown.* How many of them are you familiar with?
2. Find these cities on a map of the United States: New York, New York; Chicago, Illinois; Los Angeles, California; Pittsburgh, Pennsylvania; Dallas, Texas; Green Bay, Wisconsin. These are some of the cities that have major football teams. Given Green Bay's size and location, how do you think a victory celebration in Green Bay would differ from one in these other cities?
3. Have you ever watched the Super Bowl on TV? What is a Super Bowl party?
4. Do people in big cities in your native country have mistaken ideas about the way people live outside the city? What are some of these ideas? Is the same true of country attitudes toward the city?

As You Read

Look for the following details:
1. The writer of the first article stresses the idea that fans in Green Bay behaved differently from the way fans would behave in the other U.S. cities with big football teams. Find the details that indicate this.
2. What kinds of facts does the author of the second article point out to show the inaccuracy of the accounts in the media about the Packers and their fans?

Triumphant return to
Titletown

Packers enjoy a love-in, throngs turn out for NFL champs

By Graeme Zielinski
TRIBUNE STAFF WRITER

1 The Romans had something they called the triumph, where they would parade grandly to their ancient capital after a victory.

2 This undersized city updated that notion Monday—with a G-rated and nearly frostbitten cast—as the Green Bay Packers returned from New Orleans after winning Super Bowl XXXI Sunday over the New England Patriots 35–21.

3 In an open-air consummation of their well-documented love affair, the Packers were paraded before tens—maybe hundreds—of thousands of Wisconsinites who took to streets, snowbanks, trees and rooftops to cheer the team.

4 The spectacle confirmed the cotton-candy image the city and state have earned through its Middle American devotion.

5 Green Bay police estimated at least 100,000 people lined the 8-mile motorcade route, a number greater than the population of the city itself. And that number was in addition to a capacity crowd of more than 60,000 who paid $5 apiece to be at the end of the parade route and the players' place of business, Lambeau Field.

6 The display led Peggy Shurmur, the wife of defensive coordinator Fritz Shurmur, to wonder aloud, "Is there anyone in the town that's in their house?"

Reggie White waves to the crowd Monday night at Lambeau Field, where some 60,000 fans paid $5 each to welcome the Packers.
Photo by AP/Wide World Photos.

7 The answer was no, and the event was called "Return to Titletown" by local organizers. It took hours longer than expected because so many people wanted to feel, to touch, to see the team that dominates life in this city.

8 "If Norman Rockwell were alive, he'd be here painting a picture," said Jim Albracht, whose company manages Lambeau Field, as he looked upon those who waited hours along the parade route in a 10-below windchill.

9 The motorcade that left Austin Straubel International Airport in the early afternoon passed through town at the rate of a kidney stone, reaching peak speeds of 5 m.p.h. as fans converged on the five city buses in which the champion Packers rode.

10 "Oh, there goes my girlfriend. She wants to touch Coach (Mike) Holmgren again," said Mike Keuler, 40.

11 He trotted along with the motorcade through slushy streets as his girlfriend, Peggy Noonan, clasped the hand of the coach and other players who were embraced by the crowds.

12 "Where's Moses when you need him?" asked Nancy Haskell, the wife of a Packers coach, who was visibly stunned and pleased by the gestures of support offered up to the returning team.

13 All along the route were thousands of homespun attempts to pay tribute to the team, including messages etched in tarpaulin, cardboard, snow and construction paper. A sampling read, "I can die now," "It's Lombardi Gras" and "How 'Bout Dem Der Packers?"

14 The smallest city in the country with a professional sports team seemed interested in highlighting that distinction.

15 Schools had been let off, and most businesses closed too, while

thousands of Packer backers jammed local highways for what amounted to a pilgrimage.

16   "Holy shmoley," said 5-year-old Evan John of nearby Oneida, who commented on the thick line of cars that jammed the interstate.

17   "It's a family thing. We're a family here in Green Bay," said his father, Fran John.

18   Indeed, as large as the party grew from the hour of victory Sunday, it remained decidedly small-town.

19   For instance, about 10,000 pounds of confetti were thrown as the team wended through the downtown, launched from four buildings, none of which stood more than eight stories.

20   The night before, police reported only nine celebration-related arrests: three for disorderly conduct, three for drunken driving and three for trying to steal pennants strung up on lampposts. At the parade, and without any barricades, fans parted themselves on their own when the players' buses came through.

21   Many also clutched commemorative copies of the local papers, which read like they were written by the official Chinese news agency, saluting the team's "splendid" season and the "glorious" Super Bowl.

22   The remarkable display of affection seemed to bewilder even some of the players, who gamely endured the almost-3-hour bus ride.

23   "I, I can't believe this," said linebacker George Koonce, as he politely thanked fans along the route who would yell in his face: "Koooonce."

24   For a portion of the route, lineman John Michels walked, carrying his travel bag.

25   "Nowhere else do you have fans like this," he said. "Nowhere."

26   The self-appointed marshal of the procession became Reggie White, the popular defensive end, who rode in a fire truck at the front of the phalanx, sending the thousands into paroxysms of glee when he addressed them through a loudspeaker.

27   "Super Bowl, how 'bout that?" his disembodied voice told people, who, if they weren't holding a beer or a Packers pennant, seemed to be holding a child.

28   Gordon "Red" Batty elicited a similar response as he waggled the NFL Championship Trophy at the crowd.

29   "Incredible," said defensive lineman Santana Dotson as he boarded a bus for the parade.

30   The players weren't the only ones who expected their parade to be quicker. Lambeau Field was filled by 2 P.M., though the team didn't arrive until close to 6 P.M., sending people into restrooms and conversion vans to warm up.

31   The official ceremony was far less dramatic than the somewhat impromptu celebration that preceded it.

32   "Stay here, stay here," the fans begged of Super Bowl MVP Desmond Howard, who returned a kickoff 99 yards for a touchdown and who may leave the team for a fatter salary.

33   "It has been an extreme honor to play before you guys, the greatest fans in the world," White, an ordained minister, said, struggling to speak with lips numbed by cold.

34   Mayor Paul Jadin proclaimed the Packers "America's Team" to a crowd who already knew this.

35   And referring to a coach by the name of Lombardi who helped to distinguish this town from countless others on the American landscape, tight end Mark Chmura told the crowd, "All my teammates and myself are glad to be back in the cold weather. Vince, I know you're listening. Your trophy is safe once again."

The champs: Tens of thousands line Green Bay's streets to honor the Super Bowl champions (AP/World Wide Photos) and watch coach Mike Holmgren display the Vince Lombardi Trophy (Tribune photo by John Lee).

Nothing cheesy about Green Bay

1   Some of the recent accounts of the Green Bay Packers and their fans have left Green Bayites wondering what community is being discussed.

2   Green Bay has cold winters. It has many factories. There are millworkers in those factories. These assertions are all correct, but beyond these facts the truth has been abandoned.

3   Most of the millworkers, for example, are intelligent, hard-working people who do a lot more than go bowling, drink beer and attend Packer games. Many of them send their children to private schools. They give volunteer hours to local charities and serve on school boards. They support many cultural and educational opportunities found in Green Bay.

4   Let's get past the amusing picture that creates media hype and take a look at the real Green Bay Packers and their fans.

5   The Green Bay Packers are a community-owned team. What does that mean? It means that when the Packers were unable to meet payroll and expenses, they turned to the people of the area for support. People like my father-in-law bought shares of stock in the Packers to keep them afloat.

6   These shares of stock have been handed down to the next generation and are hanging proudly on family-room walls. Yes, the Packers are an important part of Green Bay history.

7   What often is being ignored, however, is that the same community spirit and pride that saved the Packers have given Green Bay an award-winning library and an outstanding museum. The local performing arts center brings in major talent. There is a zoo that boasts a wide variety of animals, plus a wildlife sanctuary.

8   Green Bay also has a large university and a well-respected college that are renowned for their cultural offerings and musical performances. Five of the Fortune 500's privately held companies are headquartered in Green Bay.

9   Green Bay, with the enriching, stimulating and entertaining lifestyle that it offers, has been one of the best-kept secrets in the United States. Keep on presenting the erroneous reports about life here, and it will continue to be that way.

10 In the meantime, Green Bayites will keep on growing intellectually, spiritually and athletically in an esthetically beautiful environment that few cities its size can match.

Bonnie Kaftan
DE PERE, WIS.

Chicago Tribune

Postreading

I. Getting the Message

After reading both articles, choose the best answer for each item.

1. The first article mainly
   a. describes a victory parade.
   b. explains the history of the Green Bay Packers.
   c. interviews the players of the Green Bay Packers.

2. In the first article the crowd along the victory parade route
   a. encouraged the players to move quickly.
   b. was well-behaved.
   c. was a problem for the police.

3. The author of the first article reports that the players themselves
   a. were annoyed by the fans.
   b. ignored the fans.
   c. enjoyed the fans.

4. The author of the first article mentions the fact that thousands of people waited hours in the cold in order to
   a. indicate the poor climate of Wisconsin.
   b. indicate the Green Bay fans' love for their team.
   c. show how poorly the parade was planned.

5. Most of the details that the author of the second article mentions show that
   a. Wisconsin people are serious and sophisticated.
   b. Wisconsin people are smarter than city people.
   c. Wisconsin people have the habits of farming people.

Check your answers with the key on page 165. If you have made mistakes, reread the article to gain a better understanding of it.

II. Expanding Your Vocabulary

A. Getting Meaning from Context

Find each word in the paragraph indicated in parentheses. Use context clues to determine the meaning of the word. Choose the best definition.

First Article

1. throngs (subtitle)   a. large crowd   b. athletes
2. spectacle (4)   a. sport   b. grand public show
3. motorcade (5, 9)   a. parade of vehicles   b. a special road
4. peak (9)   a. highest point   b. like a mountain
5. slushy (11)   a. full of holes   b. full of partly melted snow
6. stunned (12)   a. bored   b. surprised
7. homespun (13)   a. made at home   b. attractive
8. confetti (19)   a. tiny pieces of paper   b. decorations
9. impromptu (31)   a. organized, planned   b. without preparation, at once

Postreading

Second Article

1. assertions (2)	a. false statements	b. forceful statements
2. renowned (8)	a. disregarded	b. known and admired
3. stimulating (9)	a. exciting the mind	b. relaxing to the mind
4. erroneous (9)	a. untrue	c. evil

B. Reading for Suggested Meanings

1. The author of the first article describes the motorcade as moving at the "rate of a kidney stone" (9). A kidney stone moves very slowly and sometimes very painfully through the body. Do you think this is a good way to describe the motorcade? Why or why not?

2. The term *pilgrimage* means a journey made to a holy place. Why does the writer of the first article describe the motorcade as a *pilgrimage* (15)?

3. The author of the first article uses the term *phalanx* (26). This word had a special meaning in the armies of ancient Greece and Rome. Look up the word in a dictionary. Why is this word used to describe the crowd?

4. The writer of the second article uses the term *media hype* (4) to indicate the way television, radio, and newspapers portrayed the Green Bay Packers and their fans. This term refers to the news reports, personality profiles, feature stories, and advertising that surround films, TV shows, new consumer products, and special events. Does the term have positive or negative connotations? Why? Can you think of other examples of media hype?

III. Working with Idioms and Expressions

Study the meanings of these idioms and expressions. A form of each one appears in the indicated paragraph of the article.

First Article

love-in (subtitle) a peaceful public gathering held to demonstrate mutual love

turn out (subtitle) to come out for a public event

G-rated (2) clean, wholesome (a term taken from movie ratings)

cotton-candy image (4) innocent

offered up (12) given to (in religion, prayers are *offered up* to God)

pay tribute to (13) honor, show admiration for

paroxysms of glee (26) sudden outbursts

warm up (30) become warm

"It's Lombardi Gras" (13) a play on words combining *Lombardi* and *Mardi Gras*, a famous New Orleans celebration

"How 'Bout Dem Der Packers?" (13) makes gentle fun of the Wisconsin accent, a pronunciation of "How about them there Packers?"

"Holy shmoley" (16) a variant of "Holy smoke," indicating surprise, as in "wow."

Postreading

Second Article
keep them afloat (5) help them stay financially stable
hand down (6) to give from parents to children to grandchildren and so on
keep on (10) continue

Complete the following sentences using the idioms and expressions above and on page 58.

1. Because of their great love for the Packers, more people decided to _____ for the celebration than actually lived in the city of Green Bay.

2. Green Bay has a _____ because it is small and midwestern and is thought not to have the evils that a big city would have.

3. Because the fans were so happy, the mere sight of the team players brought on _____ .

4. After standing for hours in the cold, many of the fans probably had to _____ in their homes afterwards.

5. When the fans _____ their shouts of praise, the players felt happy and honored.

6. If the Chicago Bears were in financial trouble, would the owners sell stock to fans to _____?

IV. Talking and Writing

Discuss the following topics. Then choose one of them to write about.

1. What sports heroes from the United States or from your native country do you admire? Why do you admire them?
2. Is there any sports event in your native country that has the kind of national appeal that the Super Bowl does for people in the United States?
3. How do crowds of celebrating sports fans behave in your country? Would they act like the people of Green Bay?
4. The author of the first article says that the stories in local newspapers about the victory "read like they were written by the official Chinese news agency" (paragraph 21). This means that he thinks they were biased in favor of the Green Bay team. Does your local newspaper report team victories this way? Why or why not?
5. The letter to the editor discusses the mistaken way that television and newspapers present Wisconsin life. What kinds of misconceptions do you think Wisconsinites might have about Chicagoans? Explain.

Chicago Tribune

Preparation

How far south does Packerland go?

Previewing the Article

At first glance, this editorial seems rather odd. Most editorials are about politics, and readers turn to them to know what the newspaper officially says about various questions, such as "Who should be elected?" or "Should a particular bill be made a law?"

This editorial, however, is not political at all, and it is not even very serious. It congratulates the city of Green Bay on the victory of the Packers in the Super Bowl and is written in a light, joking tone.

Strangely enough, this kind of topic is exactly what loyal editorial readers expect, for they want their daily newspaper to comment on anything of importance to the community, especially anything that they themselves might discuss. The victory of the Packers, a long-time rival of the Chicago Bears, was very widely discussed. Chicagoans were proud that a nearby city had won the game but were a little embarrassed that such a small city had won an award that Chicago, with all its world prominence, could not win.

An editorial is more than just the official opinion of a newspaper; it is the voice of the community. People want to see their feelings expressed in print, and editorials can do this in a pleasing way.

Before You Read

Discuss the following questions:
1. Read the headline. What do you think it means? Can you rewrite the question in different words?
2. Do you read newspaper editorials? Why or why not?
3. Is there a sports rivalry between two cities in your native country? Describe it.

As You Read

As you read, look for reasons why Chicagoans think of their city as "superior" to Green Bay.

How far south does Packerland go?

1   In congratulating the people of Wisconsin on the Green Bay Packers' Super Bowl victory, we can say that we know just how they feel. Really, we do. Chicago had a Super Bowl champion once.

2   It was just 11 years ago. The Bears won under the immortal Mike Ditka, who's still so respected that he's expected to be hired to coach the New Orleans Saints despite a four-year absence from the NFL. Beat the Patriots too. We're not joking. You could look it up.

3   Of course, it could be said that we can't fully appreciate what this means to Cheeseheads. (Thanks to those Swiss-cheese hats the Packers have inspired, Wisconsinites don't even take offense at that term anymore.)

Residents of Chicagoland have so much to distract them from mere sports—from the symphony to one of the world's premier universities to the Sears Tower, which used to be the world's tallest building and is still taller than any grain silo between here and Ontario. Aside from the Packers, Wisconsin has, well, a lot of highly productive dairy cows.

4   People around here are trying to be gracious, but many of us recall fondly when the Bears were the terror of the Central Division, regularly mauling squads of hapless no-names from Green Bay. That seems a long time distant from this season, when the 7–9 Bears lost their two games against the Pack by a combined score of 65–23.

5   Some of us, though, have gone beyond gracious. One local recalls that when his kindergartner son inexplicably became a Packers fan three years ago, he had to search high and low to find a green-and-gold garment to satisfy a Christmas wish. Lately, you're as likely to see kids on Halsted Street or Roosevelt Road wearing Brett Favre's jersey as Erik Kramer's. And face it, these Packers are so well-mannered and unassuming—in contrast to last year's Super Bowl winners, the Dallas Cowboys—that they're hard to dislike.

6   No doubt most people this side of Kenosha will stick with the Milquetoasts of the Midway regardless. But Wisconsinites may forgive us if we bask in reflected glory. For a while, Chicagoans who venture southward on vacation, when asked where they're from, will be tempted to reply, "Oh, up near Green Bay."

Chicago Tribune
Postreading

I. Getting the Message

After reading the editorial, indicate if each statement is true (T) or false (F).

1. _____ The writer thinks Chicagoans should be proud of the recent record of their football team, the Bears.
2. _____ Mike Ditka is currently the coach of the Chicago Bears.
3. _____ "Cheeseheads" is a term Chicagoans use to describe people who live in Wisconsin.
4. _____ According to the article, some Chicagoans have become enthusiastic Packer fans.
5. _____ Brett Favre is a player on the Green Bay Packers.
6. _____ According to the article, the Dallas Cowboys, the winners of the previous Super Bowl, were rather unlikeable.
7. _____ The Bears and Packers played each other only once in the previous season.
8. _____ The Chicago Bears have never won the Super Bowl.

Check your answers with the key on page 165. If you have made mistakes, reread the article to gain a better understanding of it.

II. Expanding Your Vocabulary

Find each word in the paragraph indicated in parentheses. Then choose the best definition.

1. immortal (2)   a. bad, evil   b. undying
2. appreciate (3)   a. understand and enjoy   b. go up in value
3. premier (3)   a. highest quality   b. expensive
4. mauling (4)   a. hurting and treating   b. playing
                            roughly
5. hapless (4)   a. unlucky, unfortunate   b. successful
6. inexplicably (5)   a. unexplainably   b. not happily
7. garment (5)   a. toy   b. an article of clothing
8. venture (6)   a. dare to go   b. return

III. Working with Idioms and Expressions

Find each of the italicized phrases in the indicated paragraph. Choose the answer that best conveys the meaning of the phrase.

1. "Wisconsinites don't even *take offense at* that term anymore" (3) means that
   a. they don't feel insulted by the term "Cheeseheads."
   b. they don't understand what "Cheeseheads" means.
2. "... the Bears were the *terror* of the Central Division" (4) means that
   a. they were a very bad team.
   b. they were the most powerful and successful team.

Postreading

3. "...most of the people this side of Kenosha will *stick with* the Milquetoasts of the Midway regardless" (6) means that
   a. they will be loyal to the Bears.
   b. they will no longer be fans of the Bears.
4. "bask in reflected glory" (6) means
   a. be more popular and famous than Green Bay.
   b. enjoy and feel pride in the reputation of Green Bay.

IV. Analyzing Paragraphs

Reread the indicated paragraphs. Then answer the questions.
1. In paragraph 2 the editorial writer ironically boasts that Chicago won a Super Bowl "just" 11 years ago, but 11 years is clearly a long time in sports. What other words or phrases in the paragraph indicate that the writer knows that 11 years is a long time?
2. In paragraph 3 the writer seems to make fun of Wisconsin for being a farm state that lacks the benefits of a big city. But what words or phrases indicate that the writer is also making fun of Chicago?
3. The main idea of a paragraph is often given in a topic sentence. The first sentence of paragraph 5—"Some of us, though, have gone beyond gracious"—expresses the main idea, followed by supporting details. Can you rephrase this sentence in different words?
4. An old nickname for a Chicago football team is the "Monsters of the Midway." In paragraph 6 the author refers to the Bears as the "Milquetoasts of the Midway." A "milquetoast" is a timid or weak person. What is the writer indicating about the Bears and their fans in this paragraph?

V. Talking and Writing

Discuss the following topics. Then choose one of them to write about.
1. This editorial lightly makes fun of Chicago and the Chicago Bears while it addresses the people of Green Bay. This is called "self-deprecating humor," making fun of oneself. Why is this kind of humor effective? Can you think of any comedians who use self-deprecating humor?
2. Do you feel loyal to a sports team in your area? What does a feeling of loyalty to a team do for a community? Is this feeling a good thing?
3. Why do people enjoy reading about a game in the newspaper even though they saw the game itself on television the day before?

Chicago Tribune

Preparation

Failure to recognize proved costly

Previewing the Article

"Every American should say a special word of thanks to Jackie Robinson, because he proved that America is a better, stronger, richer country when we all work together." With these words President Clinton paid tribute to the first African-American major-league baseball player in the United States, Jackie Robinson of the Brooklyn Dodgers. The occasion was a ceremony commemorating the 50th anniversary of his first game played in 1947.

Before that day there were no African Americans playing on any professional team. Though slavery had ended at the time of the Civil War in the 1860s, racism and discrimination had not. African-American baseball players had their own separate baseball league and were not permitted in the National or American leagues. Jackie Robinson demonstrated that baseball or any sport is played better when it is open to all.

This feature article provides background for understanding the meaning of this anniversary. It provides facts about teams and makes an argument about the damaging effects of racism in sports. Newspapers produce a variety of stories about major news events such as this. The *Chicago Tribune,* for example, covered the ceremony itself in a news story, published various feature stories about its significance, and ran opinion essays by columnists both before and after the event.

Before You Read

Discuss the following questions:
1. What do you know about the history of the U.S. Civil Rights movement?
2. Was there ever a time when a racial or ethnic group was excluded from professional sports in your native country? Explain.
3. Is there any group of people in your native country that has had to fight for equality the way African Americans have?

As You Read

As you read, find the answer to this question: Why was it a big mistake for teams to exclude African-American athletes?

Failure to recognize
proved costly

Jackie Robinson is nipped at home plate by Cubs catcher Al Walker during an attempted steal of home at Wrigley Field on May 17, 1949.
AP/Wide World Photos.

All-white champion teams slow to change ways

By Richard Rothschild
TRIBUNE STAFF WRITER

1 They sit like a pale, forgotten exhibit in a museum, an extinct species from another time:

2 The 1953 New York Yankees, the 1953 Detroit Lions, the 1958 St. Louis Hawks, the 1959 University of California basketball team and the 1969 University of Texas football team.

3 They are the last all-white champion teams of their respective sports. And like the great beasts of old, these teams were slow to adapt when change buffeted their comfortable world.

4 Integration opened sports to all Americans but closed the minds of certain clubs and universities. Each team had its own motivation for staying white, but the end result was poorer performance.

5 Only the Yankees maintained a championship tradition, although they, too, had some learning to do. Yes, blacks such as Elston Howard, Al Downing and Hector Lopez helped the Yanks win American League pennants through 1964. But the team's failure to recognize additional African-American and Latino prospects left the cupboard bare when the great Mantle-Maris-Ford team of the early '60s crumbled with age and injury.

6 For 12 years, the Yankees wandered baseball's wilderness. When the team finally returned to postseason glory in the late 1970s the New York roster featured such black stars as Reggie Jackson, Chris Chambliss, Willie Randolph, Mickey Rivers and Roy White.

7   The Detroit Lions seemed comfortable at first with black players. The 1949 Lions had three blacks, as many as any other team in the National Football League. But one year later, the Lions had just one black; and for five of the next six seasons, no African-American could call himself a Detroit Lion.

8   Some have suggested the Lions simply were following the lead of their landlord at Tiger Stadium, the Detroit Tigers, one of the last baseball teams to integrate. Whatever the reason, the Lions, who won three NFL championships in the 1950s, have won only one postseason game since their 1957 NFL title.

9   Professional basketball integrated with fewer fireworks than the NFL and baseball but some franchises were slower than others, most notably the St. Louis Hawks. Featuring such Southern-bred stars as Bob Pettit and Cliff Hagan, the Hawks didn't think they needed blacks to succeed. In the late 1950s, they were right.

10   The Hawks won the 1958 NBA crown, after barely missing a year earlier when they were beaten in double overtime of Game 7 in the 1957 NBA Finals by the Bill

Russell–led Boston Celtics. Russell, whose draft rights originally belonged to St. Louis, had been traded to Boston for Hagan and Easy Ed Macauley in 1956.

11   Of that era, former NBA referee Norm Drucker once said: "In 1956, St. Louis was an anti-black city. The black players who played there for other (NBA) teams—the fans called them such names."

12   Ultimately, the Hawks accepted integration, and black stars such as Lenny Wilkens, Zelmo Beaty and Bill Bridges became NBA stars. But the team lost both popularity and money, eventually moving to Atlanta in 1968. The Hawks have not been back to the finals since 1961.

13   It is odd that Berkeley-based California is the last all-white NCAA basketball champ, because the community is synonymous with liberal lifestyles. And in 1955 and 1956, Russell had led Bay Area rival University of San Francisco to consecutive titles with two black teammates—K.C. Jones and Hal Perry.

14   But the Golden Bears were slow to recognize the worth of black student-athletes. As the '60s

dawned, another California university, UCLA, would attract blacks from all over the nation and build college basketball's greatest dynasty. Cal-Berkeley hasn't been back to the Final Four since 1960.

15   Texas' 1969 all-white team drew a presidential audience when Richard Nixon watched the Longhorns beat equally lily-white Arkansas in a showdown for No. 1 that December. More than two decades after Jackie Robinson broke baseball's color line, and five years after the landmark 1964 Civil Rights Law, why did Texas stick with the old ways?

16   Possibly because in Texas, football is as much a social event as it is an athletic spectacle. In the '60s, it was unlikely that well-heeled Texas alumni and coach Darrell Royal would have wanted to invite black folks to their little football party.

17   Arkansas integrated its football team a year later and Texas soon followed, but the glory road was at an end for them and their beloved Southwest Conference. Neither Texas nor any other SWC school would finish No. 1 in football. The league disbanded in 1996.

Chicago Tribune

Postreading

I. Getting the Message

After reading the article, choose the best answer for each item.

1. The main purpose of this article is to
   a. describe the struggles of black athletes.
   b. indicate that it was a mistake for teams to exclude blacks.
   c. argue that more black athletes should be in professional sports.

2. The last university to win a football championship was
   a. the University of Texas.
   b. the University of California.
   c. the University of San Francisco.

3. The author suggests that the New York Yankees were successful in the late 1970s because
   a. they had strong black players on the team.
   b. there were few black players on other teams.
   c. the number of black players was greater than the number of white players.

4. The St. Louis Hawks
   a. are now in Atlanta.
   b. were one of the first basketball teams to accept black players.
   c. have won championships often in recent years.

5. It is strange that the basketball team of the University of California at Berkeley is the last all-white NCAA champ because
   a. the community of Berkeley is not known to be racially prejudiced.
   b. the team has won more championships than any other.
   c. other teams were much more racially prejudiced.

6. In the late 1960s the University of Texas football team
   a. had many black players.
   b. had a black coach.
   c. had no black players.

7. After 1969 the University of Texas football team
   a. won 4 championships.
   b. slowly became all-black.
   c. never again won a championship.

Check your answers with the key on page 165. If you have made mistakes, reread the article to gain a better understanding of it.

II. Expanding Your Vocabulary

A. Getting Meaning from Context

Find each word in the paragraph indicated in parentheses. Use context clues to determine the meaning of the word. Choose the best definition.

1. pale (1)   a. colorless   b. bright
2. extinct (1)   a. large   b. dead
3. respective (3)   a. well-liked   b. corresponding
4. buffeted (3)   a. helped   b. upset
5. prospects (5)   a. likely future players   b. extra players
6. barely (10)   a. successfully   b. almost not
7. era (11)   a. area   b. period of time
8. eventually (12)   a. immediately   b. after a while
9. consecutive (13)   a. one after another   b. resulting from

Chicago Tribune

Postreading

B. Reading for Suggested Meanings

Answer these questions. For help, reread the paragraphs indicated in parentheses.

1. When one family provides the kings and queens for a country for a period of years, the family is a "dynasty." What is meant by referring to UCLA as basketball's "greatest dynasty" (14)?

2. In a card game, a "showdown" takes place when the players lay down their cards to show each other what cards they have been holding. The player with the best hand wins. In a football "showdown" (15) two rival teams make their best efforts to defeat the other. Find which of the following words is *not* a synonym for "showdown": *climax, tribute, crisis, clash*.

3. Literally, a "well-heeled" person is one whose shoes have nice, new heels that aren't worn down by use. Would a "well-heeled" (16) alumnus be a rich person or an average-income person?

III. Working with Idioms and Expressions

Study the meanings of the idioms and expressions below. A form of each one appears in the paragraphs indicated in parentheses.

close the mind (4) cause someone to refuse to think about something

leave the cupboard bare (5) have no supplies left

wander the wilderness (6) work and be active without success

follow the lead (8) doing the same as

stick with (15) continue despite resistance

Special Terms:

pennant (5) in major-league baseball, the championship of either the National League or the American League; the two pennant-winning teams at the end of a season play each other in the World Series

postseason game (8) one of a series of games leading to a championship played after the end of the regular season

franchise (9) a company that has official permission to operate a professional sports team

NBA (10) the National Basketball Association

overtime (10) an additional period of time to decide the winner of a tied game

draft (10) the system used in professional sports in which each team receives some of the best players

NCAA (13) the National College Athletic Association

title (13) the championship

Chicago Tribune

Postreading

Complete the sentences below with idioms and expressions from the list on page 68.

1. Teams that did not _____ of those which hired talented black players eventually hurt their own chances of success.

2. Games that go into _____ because of a tie at the end of the game are usually very exciting.

3. The New York Yankees were successful in the late 1970s in part because they decided not to

   _____ the discriminatory practices that were in place in the early 1960s.

4. University basketball coaches have to make sure that they follow rules made by the _____ .

IV. Making Sense of Sentences

Answer the following questions about the article. Make inferences when necessary.
1. The all-white teams are compared to "the great beasts of old" that were "slow to adapt" (3). What are these "beasts," and what did they have to adapt to?
2. The Yankees "had some learning to do" (5). What did they have to learn? Did they learn it?
3. "Professional basketball integrated with fewer fireworks than the NFL and base-ball" (9). Does this mean that integration in basketball was rather difficult or rather peaceful?
4. The Berkeley community in California is "synonymous with liberal lifestyles" (13). Does this mean that the area is racially prejudiced or not?
5. UCLA built its basketball dynasty "as the '60s dawned" (14). Does this mean in the early part of the sixties or the later part?

V. Talking and Writing

Discuss the following topics. Then choose one of them to write about.
1. Jackie Robinson was the first to "break the color barrier" in baseball. Can you think of other figures in other fields—like film, music, business, or politics—who crossed this barrier and are admired by all groups? Describe their accomplishments.
2. Can you think of any other areas besides sports where progress has been held back by excluding certain groups of people? Explain.

Chicago Tribune

Focus on Culture

Setting the Scene

How important are sports in the United States? A brief glimpse at any U.S. daily newspaper shows how much readers love sports. Normally the front page contains some reference to a sports story inside. Sometimes, on occasions such as the World Series, the Super Bowl, or the Olympics, sports stories are the lead articles. There are even articles on sports that are out of season and articles analyzing games days after the game has been played.

Which sports are important in the United States? This is a very different question. Though many sports, such as those featured in Olympic events, are popular all over the world, particular sports differ greatly in popularity from culture to culture. The most obvious example is American football, which is rarely played anywhere else in the world, but there are others. For example, though basketball is played all over the world, few countries can match the feverish popularity it enjoys in the United States.

Many newspaper readers turn to the sports section even before they read other news. They want to know the results of games played by their favorite teams or find out more information about games they watched on television the previous day. They also enjoy reading feature stories, favorite columnists, and news about the business of sports: Did player X sign a contract with the team? How much money is the contract worth?

Exercise 1. What's Popular?

Look through the sports section of a large Sunday edition of your local newspaper and list the four sports most frequently written about. Then, with a group, record the answers to the following questions on the chart below: 1. What is the sport? 2. How many articles are about this sport? 3. How many articles are reports about games? 4. How many are features or opinion columns? 5. How many stories are about amateur and how many are about professional sports?

	Sport	Number of Articles	Number of Reports	Number of Features or Columns	Amateur	Pro
1.						
2.						
3.						
4.						

Focus on Culture

Exercise 2. What Are the Key Issues?

Which sport in Exercise 1 had the greatest number of articles written about it? Write the headlines of three of the articles and answer these questions.

1. Do you understand the headline? What words did you have to look up?
2. Is there another article in the section on the same game or team or sports figure?
3. Can you summarize the article in one sentence?
4. Does a photo accompany the article? If so, what does it show?
5. Does the article mention any financial issues, such as player salary or team profits?
6. Does the article speculate about the future of the athlete or team?
7. If an article appeared in your native country about such an event or person, would the article be similar? Would it be different in any way? How?
8. What do these similarities and differences tell you about sports in the United States?

Exercise 3. The Language of Sports

The sports section contains some of the liveliest writing in the newspaper. For this reason, the vocabulary can sometimes be a little difficult for learners of English. For example, when a sports headline reports that a team won a game, it seldom uses a colorless word like *win*. It is likely to use more vivid words like *edge*, *sweep*, *pound*, *thrash*, *trounce*, *bury*, *rout*, or *hammer*. Furthermore, each sport has its own special terminology.

For this exercise, pick a sport that you know. Look at several newspaper articles about the sport. Make a list of terms related to the sport. Arrange them in categories such as the ones listed below. Add or delete categories as appropriate.

positions on the field	
plays	
verbs (action words)	
slang	
idioms	
other	

Share your list with your classmates. Compare your list with those of other students who chose the same sport.

Chicago Tribune

Focus on Culture

Exercise 4. Understanding a Profile

An important value in the United States is *individualism*—the belief that an individual can achieve success against great odds. All sports—even team sports—provide a stage for the success stories of talented individuals. The life stories of Michael Jordan in basketball, Tiger Woods in golf, Jackie Robinson in baseball, and many others are well known to U.S. sports fans. Of course, not all profiles are positive. Sometimes an athlete is portrayed negatively, as having played or behaved badly.

For this exercise find an article that tells the story of a sports figure and answer these questions:
1. Who is the athlete and what is the sport?
2. Why is the athlete profiled?
3. Does the article portray the athlete sympathetically or unsympathetically?
4. Do you agree with the author of the article?
5. Does the article make you want to read more about this person? Why or why not?

Exercise 5. Journal Assignment: Follow Your Team

Pick a local team that is currently playing several televised games a week and whose games are always covered by your local newspaper. For example, basketball, baseball, and hockey play games with great frequency. Watch one of the games on TV and then read the account of the game the following day. Then write a journal entry that answers the following questions:
1. What teams played?
2. What was the score?
3. Does the newspaper account add to your understanding of the game you saw? Does it make you more familiar with the players?
4. Does the article express any opinions that you disagree with?
5. Does reading the article actually add to your appreciation of the sport? Why or why not?

Then watch the following game, read the next article, and answer the same questions.

Chicago Tribune

SectionFive

Food&Restaurants

Focus on Culture

Food and Restaurants

Chicago Tribune

Food&Restaurants

As American As Apple Pie

Used for things that are really "American," the expression in the title today seems out of date. We could just as well say, "as American as tacos, or take-out Chinese, or Chicago-style pizza." These three dishes—connected to Mexico, China, and Italy—are so common and so "American" that fast-food chains serve them to drivers who don't even get out of their cars. Since the first Thanksgiving, when Native Americans shared their corn with the Pilgrims, American cuisine has been a wonderful mix of many culinary traditions.

What people in the United States eat is as various as the cultures of the country, though some foods, like hamburgers and hot dogs, seem to be symbols of American dining. How people eat is another matter. Many value the tradition of the family dinner at home. They value the ideal of a close, traditional family eating dinner together each evening and sharing the experiences of the day in spirited conversation. But these days, very few families have schedules that permit eating together: the children may have after-school activities that go past dinnertime, both parents may work until early in the evening, or there may be only one parent in the household and thus no time for cooking. So people turn to three quick solutions: buying prepared foods at the supermarket, ordering out, and eating out.

Daily newspapers reflect these three solutions. Many readers study their local paper for supermarket ads and coupons to save money and find discounts. The typical supermarket provides not only prepared and frozen foods but also fully cooked dinners to take home. Restaurants also advertise heavily in the newspaper, and restaurant reviews help readers decide where to go for a night out. Franchise restaurants—national chains like McDonald's, Burger King, and Taco Bell—are the result of this need for a fast, convenient alternative to a home-cooked dinner.

But the rarity of home-cooked dinners makes them even more special. As a result, when people in the United States do cook a meal, they frequently turn to the food sections and recipes in the local newspapers in order to make something especially tasty. And the popularity of low-calorie and low-fat recipes is a response to the fact that people do less and less active manual work and are increasingly overweight. Thus dieting is popular as well. Americans like to think of their country as a land of plenty—plenty of jobs and natural resources and farm land, but also endless cheeseburgers, pizza, hot dogs, and carry-out.

Chicago Tribune

Preparation

What! No turkey?

Previewing the Article

"You are what you eat." This expression seems truest on Thanksgiving, the most important holiday of the year for a festive family meal. The rituals of this day—what people do, when they do it, what dishes are served—take on great emotional importance. When any change is made in a traditional dish, people can become upset. The repetition of holiday routines is comforting to people and is part of how they think of themselves.

The first Thanksgiving, in 1621, differed greatly from the celebration of today. In a historic meeting of cultures, English Puritans and Native Americans gathered together peacefully and ate a variety of foods that were new to them. But what started with tolerance of differences has become a tradition based on a menu that is almost always the same. Turkey, dressing, pumpkin pie, and cranberry sauce are a few of the basics, but each family has foods that individual members fiercely cling to. A tiny, unexpected addition to a recipe—such as raisins in the stuffing—can make people behave in a way that would surely surprise the early Pilgrims.

The following notes will help you understand the article:

- *Norman Rockwell* (1894–1978) was a popular illustrator who depicted American life in humorous, sentimental, and somewhat idealized ways.
- *The Boston Tea Party* is the name of a famous protest by colonial Americans just before the American Revolution.
- *DNA* is the acid (deoxyribonucleic acid) that carries genetic information to a cell.
- *Redi-Whip* is the brand name of a ready-to-use whipped cream.

Before You Read

Discuss the following questions:
1. Have you ever eaten a traditional American Thanksgiving meal? Were there any dishes that you particularly enjoyed?
2. At special holiday meals in your native country, do changes to the menu upset people?
3. Have you ever seen the pictures of the famous American illustrator Norman Rockwell? For many years his paintings of ordinary Americans appeared on the covers of a number of U.S. magazines.

As You Read

As you read, look for answers to the following questions:
1. What is a mother's role in creating or changing a Thanksgiving family tradition?
2. How many people are quoted in the article? Are there enough people to make the point the author wants to make?

Messing with
Thanksgiving
traditions
can mean
more than just
changing
the menu

WHAT!
No turkey?

By Pat Dailey
TRIBUNE STAFF WRITER

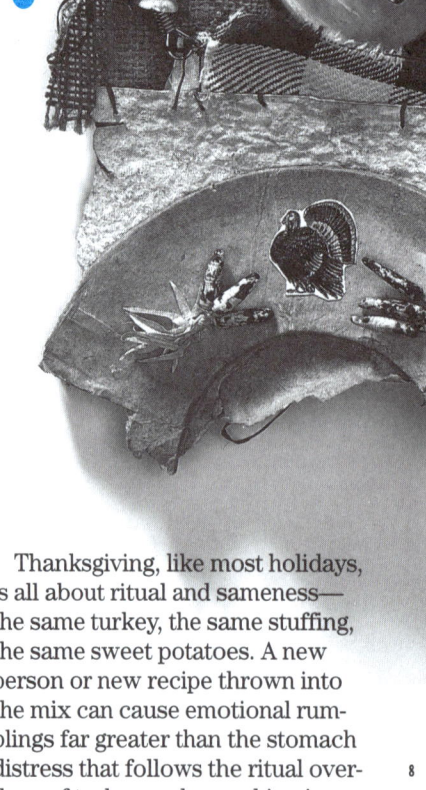

Illustration by
Susan Leopold

1   Call it the raisin rebellion, a fateful day several years back, when Brian Bonebrake's family gathered around the Thanksgiving table, expecting that tradition would once again be the guiding force behind the meal.

2   Sure enough, everything seemed just about as cheery and perfect as a Norman Rockwell painting until close examination revealed shriveled black specks in the stuffing. They might as well have been Japanese beetles.

3   "She put raisins in the bread stuffing! For a thousand years, my mother has made the exact same stuffing, and all of a sudden, she puts raisins in it. She's Sicilian. Sicilians don't do that," Bonebrake says, still undone by the case of stuffing bait-and-switch.

4   "She put them in because my stepfather wanted them. He was raised in Cuba and they eat stuff like that there," he adds. "And we had to get him an armchair. We always had side chairs around the table."

5   Thanksgiving, like most holidays, is all about ritual and sameness— the same turkey, the same stuffing, the same sweet potatoes. A new person or new recipe thrown into the mix can cause emotional rumblings far greater than the stomach distress that follows the ritual overdose of turkey and pumpkin pie.

6   Just as the Boston Tea Party wasn't about orange pekoe, Bonebrake's dinner-table insurrection probably had little to do with the offending raisins. Food is invested with so many layers of emotional significance that it often provokes responses that aren't even remotely connected to nutrition or taste.

7   "Holiday associations are so strong, they're practically part of our DNA," says Ronna Kabatznick,

a social psychologist from Berkeley, Calif. "When someone throws a curve, whether it's different food, location or people, it completely uproots our sense of reality. You end up looking around and asking yourself, 'Is this really Thanksgiving?' "

8   Reality, on this particular day, is dished up on a big platter and a battalion of serving bowls. For many, a meal that's unfailingly consistent with their accrued memories is the only one worth having. And it probably has less to do with feeling a special kinship to everyone from the Pilgrims on down than it does with the comfort of familiarity.

9   "Food mirrors all of our attachments to people and events," Kabatznick says. "We really don't want any of that to change, espe-

cially at the holidays."

10 "My mother could put my (Thanksgiving) dinner on a plate right now," says Allan Van Every, a Chicago physical therapist. "I eat the same thing every year and I don't want it messed around with. Matter of fact, I know everything—the time we'll sit down, who I'll sit next to, even the exact plate she'll serve it on."

Creamed peas and onions

11 Elizabeth Barrett, a public relations executive, is so adamant about having creamed peas and onions for Thanksgiving that she brings them along, no matter where she goes for dinner.

12 "I lived in Texas for eight years and where I went, so did they. It came to be understood that if I was there, so were the peas. Then it was OK that I wasn't with my family as long as I had my vegetables," she says. "I've been eating them since I was 2 years old. They define Thanksgiving."

13 Not everyone develops the same attachments, of course, even within families. While creamed peas are Thanksgiving's big *sine qua non* for Barrett, the rest of her family's appetites reside elsewhere. Now back in Chicago, she makes a few predictions about what will be dished up to whom.

14 "Basically, my whole family eats a one-course dinner. No one else has anything to do with the peas and onions, so they're all mine. My brother insists on oyster stuffing, my sister eats sweet potatoes with icky mini-marshmallows all over the top. Dad wants pumpkin pie with raisins and a whole can of Redi-Whip. That's so gross. We tell him, 'If you want it, Dad, bring it.' And he does. We accept each other's idiosyncrasies. At least when it comes to food."

15 Turkey unites them to some extent, though. Barrett recalls the time a hapless guest proudly presented her contribution to dinner, a crown roast of pork.

16 "It was beautiful sitting there alongside the turkey, but we just stared at it like it was some alien life form. No one touched it. It was so sad. Pork with stuffing and cranberries? No way."

17 Save for an occasional ham or wayward beef roast, a big, bronzed turkey is Thanksgiving's poster child, and 90 percent of Americans will gobble the big bird today. The matter of stuffing, or dressing, is more contentious.

18 One man, who asked that his name not be used, says that in retrospect, last year's stuffing, although it signaled the end of a relationship, left him with much to be thankful for.

19 "It kind of woke me up. The whole time we went out, six years, we created our own holidays, built up all these things that were important, that you come to expect and depend on. Last year, I'm carving the turkey, digging out the stuffing. The sausage and bread stuffing we always had was replaced with cranberry rice stuffing—no warning. It sounds simplistic, but I knew something a lot bigger than the stuffing wasn't right."

That's how mom did it

20 In social contexts, food becomes a code with complex messages that speak volumes about the status of relationships. It may look as simple as a bowl of bread stuffing or cranberry relish, but it can harbor a complex stew of emotions, starting with the age-old aphorism that "food is love."

21 Katherine Lauderdale, who spent last Thanksgiving at a good friend's home, says the stuffing spat that ensued all boiled down to one thing.

22 "I was right, she was wrong," she says with unwavering certainty and nearly uncontrolled laughter, recalling that two adults spent the better part of an hour scrapping over white bread in the stuffing. The host thought more cornbread was called for and proceeded to bake a pan of it to drive home her point.

23 "I wouldn't call it screaming but we were making our points pretty aggressively. We cleared out the kitchen. Pretty soon, everyone else was huddled in the garage, trying to disappear," Lauderdale, a lawyer, recalls. "No one else wanted to have to take sides."

24 The issue was simple: One memory bumping up against another.

25 "It goes back to the way mothers make things. And my mother's is the right way," Lauderdale says, adding that she lost the battle and watched helplessly while her mother's beloved stuffing recipe was debauched.

26 "I didn't kvetch at the table or anything, but I made it perfectly clear that the stuff we ate was not my mother's recipe and that I had nothing to do with it," she says. "And by the way, I'm going back to my mother's this year."

27 Not everyone lives by such iron-clad rules. Bryan Coomes, a Paris-based photographer, has learned to endure, even appreciate change, even if it means roast turkey thighs for overseas celebrations.

28 "In France, the only time you find whole turkeys is Christmas. Otherwise, they sell these big legs with the thigh attached so we put those frilly papers on the end to make it seem festive."

29 Even turkey has flown the coop in some celebrations. Tim Hunt, a police officer assigned to the bicycle patrol unit, says that as long as he's with family, he doesn't miss that most sacred symbol a bit.

30 "I'm a vegetarian, so no more turkey, no more anything. My family has learned to be flexible," he says. This year, he'll probably spring hommous and vegetarian fajitas, made with seitan (a type of wheat meat), on his family.

31 "They're pretty flexible, at least when I'm there to defend myself. But I'm always a little suspicious that my dad grumbles about the food just as soon as I've walked out that door."

32 Kabatznick reminds that the true spirit of Thanksgiving isn't found in a plate of creamed peas and onions or Sicilian stuffing.

33 "We're the envy of everyone on the planet. Instead of getting all caught up in the horror of something that's different from your expectations, take it in stride. Just be grateful you're lucky enough to have a nice hot meal and a warm place to eat it."

Chicago Tribune

Postreading

I. Getting the Message

After reading the article, indicate if each statement is true (T) or false (F). For help reread the paragraphs indicated by the numbers in parentheses.

1. _____ A new recipe on Thanksgiving can cause problems because people have different ideas of nutrition. (6)
2. _____ People who are upset about a Thanksgiving Day meal probably aren't thinking of the American tradition dating back to the Pilgrims. (8)
3. _____ Even individuals within the same family can disagree about food choices. (13)
4. _____ The roast pork was not eaten because it didn't taste very good. (16)
5. _____ The vast majority of Americans agree that turkey should be eaten on Thanksgiving. (17)
6. _____ Katherine Lauderdale, in discussing the previous year's fight over the stuffing, showed that she knew how ridiculous the fight had been. (22)
7. _____ Bryan Coomes, who lives in Paris, is more flexible about his Thanksgiving dinner than the others interviewed in the article. (27)
8. _____ Tim Hunt, who is a vegetarian, makes an exception on Thanksgiving and eats turkey because of family pressure. (30)
9. _____ The main idea of this article is probably best expressed by the social psychologist Ronna Kabatznick: "Food mirrors all of our attachments to people and events. We really don't want any of that to change, especially at the holidays." (9)

II. Expanding Your Vocabulary

A. Getting Meaning from Context

Find each word in the paragraph indicated in parentheses. Use context clues to determine the meaning of each word. Then choose the best definition.

1. undone (3)	a. defeated	b. rewarded
2. insurrection (6)	a. distaste	b. rebellion
3. uproots (7)	a. upsets	b. reassures
4. battalion (8)	a. a large number	b. circle
5. accrued (8)	a. lessened	b. accumulated
6. adamant (11)	a. insistent	b. indifferent
7. icky (14)	a. bad-tasting	b. delicious
8. idiosyncrasies (14)	a. manners	b. odd tastes or habits
9. contentious (17)	a. causing agreement	b. causing argument
10. debauched (25)	a. ruined	b. improved

Postreading

B. Reading for Suggested Meanings

Answer these questions.

1. In paragraph 5, what is a "ritual overdose" of turkey? What does "overdose" usually refer to?
2. In paragraph 16, what word is a synonym for "eat"? Why is this word used?
3. In paragraph 17, the turkey is humorously called "Thanksgiving's poster child." A poster child is a child whose photograph is used in advertising to represent and draw attention to a medical problem. In what sense could a turkey be a "poster child"?
4. In paragraph 19 the speaker says, "It sounds simplistic," and then comments that when his friend changed the stuffing without his consent, he knew that something more important—their relationship—was wrong. What does the speaker mean by "it sounds simplistic"?
5. In paragraph 23 the dinner guests are described as "huddled" in the garage during the big fight about the stuffing. Describe a "huddled" group. What is a huddle in American football?

III. Working with Idioms and Expressions

Study the meaning of the idioms and expressions below. The paragraphs where they appear are indicated by numbers in parentheses.

bait and switch (3) a form of misleading advertising. Customers go to a store after seeing an ad for a bargain item (the bait). When they arrive at the store, a sales-person tells them that the item is inferior to a higher-priced one or says that the bargain item is sold out.

throw a curve (7) change unexpectedly and cause confusion

mess around with (10) change something and create disorder

when it comes to (14) concerning

speak volumes (20) say a great deal, reveal much

boil down to (21) mean, leaving out unnecessary elements

drive home a point (22) argue forcefully

flown the coop (29) run away

caught up in (33) get interested or involved in

take it in stride (33) accept and deal with easily

Chicago Tribune

Postreading

Use the idioms and expressions on page 79 to complete the sentences below. Be sure
to use the correct verb forms.

1. Brian Bonebrake did not react very happily to the stuffing _____.

2. The psychologist advises Americans not to get _____ their disap-

   pointment when the host suddenly _____ into their holiday ritual.

3. When one host wanted to _____ during a

   disagreement over preparation of the stuffing, she baked more cornbread.

IV. Analyzing Paragraphs

Each story tells us something about the effects of changes to the Thanksgiving ritual.
Reread the paragraphs indicated in parentheses and match the person with the idea
that the person's story illustrates. The first one has been done for you.

__D__ 1. Brian Bonebrake (1–4)   a. shows an exception—that some families can do without turkey

_____ 2. Ronna Kabatznick (7–9, 32–33)   b. shows that individuals in a family can have their own traditions

_____ 3. Elizabeth Barrett (11–16)   c. shows that some people can be flexible about the traditional
menu when they live outside the United States

_____ 4. Katherine Lauderdale (21–26)   d. introduces the issue of family clashes over changes in the
Thanksgiving menu

_____ 5. Bryan Coomes (27–28)   e. shows how intense a disagreement over a small change in food
preparation can become

_____ 6. Tim Hunt (29–31)   f. interprets the cultural and emotional aspects of the issue

Now reread paragraph 10. What does the quotation from Allan Van Every reveal about
some people's expectations about the Thanksgiving meal?

V. Talking and Writing

In a group discuss the topics below. Then choose one of them to write about.

1. In your native country is there an important holiday feast comparable to
   Thanksgiving, at which certain foods are normally served? If so, what is served at
   this meal? How would you feel if a small change were made in the menu?

2. In the United States people often discuss and evaluate the food they are eating
   during a meal. Usually, their comments about the meal are positive. Would this
   behavior be considered polite in your native country?

3. A gathering of the *extended family*—the uncles, aunts, cousins, grandparents, and
   in-laws—is uncommon in the United States. In your opinion, why is this true? How
   often do extended-family members get together in your native country?

Chicago Tribune

Preparation

The land of the bland

Previewing the Article

"It's like an entirely different culture." This statement could come from an American comparing the dining preferences of people in the suburbs and those of people in the city.

The difference between these two worlds is a fascinating highlight of the article "The Land of the Bland," which reports the results of a study by the *Chicago Tribune*. The newspaper asked ex-Chicagoans who had moved to the suburbs what they missed most about the city. People most commonly said they missed the restaurants. After all, the multiethnic neighborhoods of Chicago have a wealth of restaurants where Chicagoans can take a small tour of the world just by eating out. They can sample Greek, Ethiopian, Korean, Indian, Mexican, or almost any other cuisine any night of the week. They can also dine elegantly or cheaply on ribs, steak, or vegetarian dishes.

Many suburbanites, however, see dining out differently. They prefer the more predictable dishes of a national chain with a standard menu, like Pizza Hut or Chi Chi's, which are typically on a highway or in a mall. Driving out to eat is quite different from the city experience of walking a couple of blocks to a Pakistani or Peruvian restaurant. People who move away from the city for the advantages of the suburbs feel the loss of the excitement and neighborliness that small city restaurants bring.

Before You Read

Discuss the following questions:

1. What was your favorite restaurant in the city or town that you come from? Why did you like this restaurant?
2. Do people in your native country frequently go out to eat? Why or why not?
3. How often do you eat in a restaurant? What sort of restaurant do you usually prefer?
4. Two kinds of restaurants mentioned in this article are national franchises or chain restaurants—like Pizza Hut or Burger King—and small local restaurants that are not part of a national company. What are the peculiar benefits of each kind of restaurant?

As You Read

Try to answer this question: What do the ex-Chicagoans regard as the social benefits of eating out at a city restaurant?

The land of the bland

Suburban thoroughfares, such as Ogden Avenue in Naperville, may be loaded with restaurants, but many city expatriates doubt if they're worth the hassle and the traffic. Tribune photo by Milbert Orlando Brown.

By Phil Vettel
TRIBUNE RESTAURANT CRITIC

1   Those planning to move out of Chicago should be warned: Others have left, only to find their new surroundings difficult to digest.

2   As part of a yearlong study of why people move out of Chicago, the Tribune surveyed the adults in almost 3,000 households who left for the suburbs and beyond between April 1 and Oct. 31, 1992. Among other questions, the survey asked which aspects of Chicago they missed most.

3   Overwhelmingly, they said they missed their favorite restaurants. Whether it's that cozy neighborhood place around the corner, the romantic spot downtown or the carryout shack that just happens to dish out the world's greatest pizza, restaurants are an inseparable part of Chicago living, part of what makes the city so vibrant and exciting.

4   And when Chicagoans move, they generally leave those restaurants for good. In follow-up interviews to the survey, some respondents said they missed the number and variety of Chicago's ethnic restaurants. Others focused on the caliber of Chicago's restaurants, bemoaning the lack of similar quality in their new towns. Many, particularly those who once lived in the Near North, Lincoln Park or Lakeview neighborhoods, missed the convenience of living in an area where dozens of good restaurants were within easy walking distance. Denise Yocum, who moved to Bolingbrook from Lincoln Park, said that in the old days, dozens of restaurants were just steps away.

5   "When I'd want pizza, I'd order depending on the kind of pizza I wanted," she said. "Stuffed, it was Bacino's; thin crust, I'd order somewhere else. I'd go to Renalli's to sit and eat, other places for delivery. There was just so much variety. I haven't found one pizzeria (out here) that is convenient and tastes good. There are a few in Naperville that aren't too bad, but they won't deliver that far (to Bolingbrook). And the suburbs' idea of a Mexican restaurant is Chi-Chi's. It's OK, but not anywhere near as good as the places I used to go to.

6   "I would love it if they just had some great restaurants nearby. I'm not really a picky eater, but once you have food that's good, and you move somewhere where they don't have it—I mean, you move to a small town and their idea of a good pizza is Pizza Hut, it's kind of a joke."

7   Nearly two-thirds of Chicagoans who leave settle in the suburbs, and many find their new environs to be a culinary wasteland when it comes to ethnic restaurants.

8   "I can't find a decent Thai restaurant out here," said Carole Schmidt, 32, of Bloomingdale, with more than a trace of disgust in her voice. "I can't find any ethnic restaurants. That's the thing about the burbs; even the things that call themselves ethnic, like

Mexican and Chinese, turn out to be Americanized Mexican or sweet-and-sour Chinese."

9 Schmidt said that when she and her husband lived in Chicago, they'd often go on culinary safaris. "We'd just explore. We'd go into a different neighborhood, close to public transportation—we didn't own a car for 10 years—and search out these mom-and-pops with 10 tables. We would find little places that not everybody knows about."

10 Now, she said, "it's fighting lights and traffic on Army Trail Road. To go through all that to get mediocre food—why? That's why we're learning to cook."

11 When she lived in Chicago, Schmidt said, she used different restaurants for specific social purposes. "The Red Tomato, up on Southport, was sort of our late-evening, friends-trickle-in, dining-gathering spot. People we hadn't seen in weeks would all meet and eat at 9:30, 10 at night. Just laugh and catch up and tell stories.

12 "I miss . . . Angelina's, on Broadway," she said. "It's fun, and kind of chaotic; you're almost touching the people seated next to you. And Heartland Cafe; I desperately miss the Heartland Cafe. That's for the granola-head side of my personality."

A social setting

13 Bev Dunham, who now lives in Oak Forest and soon will move to Tinley Park, has another gripe about the dining scene outside Chicago.

14 "People don't talk," she said. "Go to any restaurant, and you don't see people talking. In the city, even if you're by yourself there's always some conversation to get involved in. People talk.

15 "In the city, dining out is an experience. It's fun. You notice a single person in a restaurant (in the city), you don't feel bad about saying, 'Gee, I noticed you're by yourself; would you like some company?'

16 "Out here, you don't dare do that. Nobody talks to you in a restaurant. Out here, people go to restaurants just to eat. They're hungry and they want something fast. It's a real big difference. It's like an entirely different culture."

17 Dunham said the Chicago restaurants she misses aren't fancy but are social places with good food. "I used to love Mongolian House—absolutely the greatest Szechwan you'll find—and naturally everybody loves (Pizzeria) Uno and Due. I liked Hy's of Canada when it was open. And I like the Indian restaurants, even though as soon as I get a favorite one, they move.

18 "My favorite was the Diner, a block west of Ashland and Irving Park. It's a down-home place—you can't even get ice for the ice water—but the people are neat. So if you want the chili and the hot sauce and just want to be there with the guys from the neighborhood, it's great. Especially after 2 A.M." Christine Zrinsky and Michael Mach used to live in a convenient but tiny apartment in Streeterville. When they began house hunting, they found the affordable houses were a long way from the Loop, where they work.

19 They ended up in Wheaton. "We figured as long as it was going to take 45 minutes to get to work, we might as well have the property," Zrinsky said. "But we didn't think about restaurants, really, when we were going through the (house-hunting) process," she said. "We were just looking to get a home close to the train. We figured there'd be restaurants around. It's just a given in the city that you'd have restaurants nearby, and that's not the case out here."

20 Zrinsky and Mach, who passed more top-flight restaurants walking home each night in the city than most collar counties can lay claim to, discovered that good restaurants were harder to find in the suburbs. "We have found a few, but it has been hard," Mach said. "It's not quite as convenient to get to quality restaurants. Garardo's (in Naperville) is quite a drive from our neck of the woods. I'm not yet in sync with the suburban driving ethic. I miss being able to walk off those big meals."

Forget pizza in San Francisco

21 So suburbia is something short of culinary heaven. But even moving into a city with a reputation for good restaurants is no guarantee of dining bliss. "Yes, it's possible to miss Chicago restaurants when you live in San Francisco," said Kevin Gooding, a former North Sider who left last year. "They have great restaurants in San Francisco, but I can't afford them. Entree prices are $2 to $3 more; that adds up. And I notice in the Mexican restaurants, what's $6 or $7 in Chicago is $10 or $11 here.

22 "And I can't find my pizza. That's the No. 1 thing. My favorite was Giordano's stuffed pizza. Out here they have one of the Pizzeria Uno chain stores, but that's it."

23 "Actually," said Otta Ramos, a former Lakeview resident who moved to restaurant-rich Los Angeles, "the restaurant selection here is very good. You can find pretty much anything. But I was happy with the selection in Chicago.

24 "Like Gino's," Ramos said, referring to Original Gino's East. "They don't have deep-dish pizza out here. Gino's East was always a fun place to go eat."

25 "I haven't missed much," said Preston J. Edwards, who left Chicago's West Side for New Orleans, also well stocked with restaurants. "New Orleans has Chicago beat hands down in the number of seafood restaurants, and the number of good ones. Seafood costs a lot less here too.

26 "On the other hand, no one (in New Orleans) can handle Carson's. New Orleans doesn't have any rib restaurants as good. And the Chinese and Italian restaurants aren't nearly as good.

27 "I get my fill (of Chicago food) when I come back for visits," he said. "That's what we did the last time we were back—all we ate was Chinese and Carson's."

Chicago Tribune

Postreading

I. Getting the Message

After reading the article, choose the best answer for each item.

1. According to this article, most people who move away from Chicago
   a. find better restaurants in the suburbs.
   b. miss their favorite restaurants in the city.
   c. drive back into the city often to eat in their favorite restaurants.

2. A common complaint of those who move to the suburbs is
   a. that they must now drive to eat at a restaurant.
   b. that the restaurants are all too small where they live.
   c. that fast food is now harder to obtain.

3. Most of the favorite city restaurants that the ex-Chicagoans mention are
   a. easy to reach.
   b. fancy and expensive.
   c. places where only students go.

4. A frequently mentioned favorite food item in the article is
   a. Chicken Kiev.
   b. cheeseburgers.
   c. pizza.

5. One aspect of city restaurants that some ex-Chicagoans mention in the article is
   a. the peace and quiet.
   b. the friendly, lively atmosphere.
   c. the new beautiful decorations.

6. According to some ex-Chicagoans, a very good place to find ethnic restaurants—that is, restaurants that serve the particular food of a foreign country—is
   a. Chicago.
   b. the suburbs.
   c. the small towns away from the suburbs.

Check your answers with the key on page 166. If you have made mistakes, reread the article to gain a better understanding of it.

II. Expanding Your Vocabulary

Find each word in the paragraph indicated in parentheses. Use context clues to determine the meaning of the word. Choose the best definition.

1. surveyed (2)   a. demanded, urged   b. studied, asked
2. overwhelmingly (3) a. by a large majority b. by a small part
3. cozy (3)   a. fancy, expensive   b. warm, comfortable
4. caliber (4)   a. size   b. quality
5. settle (7)   a. go and live   b. eat
6. mediocre (10)   a. the best   b. average
7. specific (11)   a. particular   b. correct
8. gripe (13)   a. compliment   b. complaint
9. bliss (21)   a. correctness   b. happiness

Chicago Tribune

Postreading

III. Working with Idioms and Expressions

Study the meanings of the idioms and expressions below. The paragraphs where they
appear are indicated by numbers in parentheses.

leave for good (4) go away and not come back

just steps away (4) very close

picky eater (6) a person who only eats certain foods and won't eat others

mom and pops (9) small stores or restaurants owned by individuals

granola-head (12) a person who eats healthy food

house hunting (18) searching for a house to buy

collar counties (20) counties that lie next to the borders of a big city

lay claim to (20) declare ownership

neck of the woods (20) residential area

in sync with (20) in harmony with

walk off (20) take a walk after a big meal; not to be confused with *walk off with
    something,* which means "to steal something"

beat hands down (25) win easily

Complete the sentences below with the idioms and expressions above.

1. When ex-Chicagoans compare restaurants in the city with restaurants in the suburbs, the city restaurants

    have the suburban ones _____ .

2. Large, fancy restaurants have much more room for customers than the small _____ do.

3. Chicago can _____ a large number of ethnic restaurants, but a small town can't.

4. _____ is a necessity for people who want to move out of an apartment or condominium.

IV. Talking and Writing

Discuss the questions below. Then choose one of them to write about.
1. The people interviewed in this article miss the restaurants of the city, but they still
   prefer to live in the suburbs. What do you think some of the advantages of living
   in the suburbs are?
2. Do people in your native culture enjoy lively conversation at a meal in a restaurant? Is this the same for them as at a meal at home? Explain.
3. Are people from your own culture interested in the ethnic food of other countries?
   Do you think it is a good thing to know about and enjoy various ethnic foods?
   Why or why not?
4. Do you prefer dining at a national chain restaurant or a small local one? Why?

Chicago Tribune

Focus on Culture

Setting the Scene

Everybody eats, so everybody is interested in food. And newspapers have much to provide readers who are hungry for information about food. In fact, getting information about food is one of the most practical uses that readers make of their newspapers. This information is provided in several different ways:

1. Recipes: These can be of many kinds. Some are appropriate for particular seasons or holidays. Others are ethnic, gourmet, or party recipes. Still others are for side dishes, desserts, drinks, breakfasts, brunches, barbecues, and any other occasions.

2. Restaurant reviews: Much like theater or film reviews, these evaluate the restaurant from the personal point of view of the reviewer. They usually discuss the quality of the food, the decor, and the service.

3. Advertisements for food stores and restaurants: Food store ads are often full-page or even full-color pull-out sections. Restaurant ads are less frequent and smaller.

4. Coupons for discounts at food stores: These are so useful that some people buy the newspaper mainly to cut these out and use them. They usually appear in a Sunday edition.

5. Feature stories: These are articles that can be about trends in cooking, the popularity of certain restaurants, or profiles of restaurant owners or celebrity cooks. They may analyze certain American eating habits or traditions.

6. Tips for entertaining: These are "how-to" articles that give directions for giving parties at certain key holidays.

7. News stories: Stories about crop failures, new soft drinks, fast food chains, and new dangers discovered in the ingredients in certain foods are very common. Unlike the content of the rest of the newspaper—such as news reports, political analysis, and opinion columns—the above items about food often have direct, practical uses: to save money, to plan a meal, to have a satisfying dinner in a restaurant, to eat in a healthier way.

Exercise 1. Newspaper Search

Many newspapers have a special food section that appears one day a week. In the *Chicago Tribune,* for example, the food section appears every Thursday. In addition, many supermarkets advertise heavily on Sunday, some with their own full-color pages with coupons for special sale items. And a special Friday section lists restaurants.

Scan your local newspaper for several days for the following items. Then briefly note the information on page 87 and, with a group of classmates, discuss what you have found.

Chicago Tribune

Focus on Culture

1. Restaurant Review

   Name of restaurant: _____

   Type of restaurant: _____

   Would such an article appear in a newspaper in your native country? _____

2. Dessert Recipe

   Name of dessert: _____

   Would you like to try this recipe yourself? _____

   Is this a common dessert item in your native country? _____

3. Advertisement for a Supermarket

   Name of supermarket: _____

   Do the prices seem reasonable or too expensive? _____

   Do you shop there? Why or why not? _____

4. General Feature Article on a Food or Restaurant Topic

   Headline: _____

   Topic: _____

   Would such an article appear in a newspaper in your native country? _____

Exercise 2. The American Dilemma: Fitness or Fatness?

Food production in the United States has had an unfortunate result: according to a recent study, 37 percent of Americans are severely overweight. People in the United States love to eat but dream of being thin, fit, and youthful. A walk down any supermarket aisle reveals this tendency: many prepared food products are labeled "fat free," "low fat," "low calorie," and "salt free."

For this exercise, find coupons or ads for prepared or frozen food items sold at supermarkets and cut them out. These foods come in a box or bag and could be whole dinners, breakfast cereal, or snack items. Write down the brand names of four foods that are advertised as healthful or diet food and the brand names of four that are not. Complete the charts on page 88 with the following information: (1) what healthful features the foods claim to have (such as low-calorie, low-salt, low-fat, or added vitamins); (2) what the unhealthful features of the other foods seem to be (such as high sugar, fat, or salt content); (3) whether or not you have ever bought the item; and (4) whether or not you would like to try it.

Chicago Tribune

Focus on Culture

A. Fit: Healthful Prepared Foods

	Brand Name	Healthful Feature	Have you ever bought it?	Would you like to buy it?
1.				
2.				
3.				
4.				

B. Fat: Not Very Healthful Prepared Foods

	Brand Name	Unhealthful Feature	Have you ever bought it?	Would you like to buy it?
1.				
2.				
3.				
4.				

Exercise 3. Just Do It!

Skim the recipes in your local newspaper for ones that look delicious but you have never tried before. Choose one and carefully look over the list of ingredients. Be sure to note all the words that may be unfamiliar to you. Next, go to a grocery store and buy any ingredients that you don't already have. Finally, prepare the recipe and enjoy!

Exercise 4. Journal Assignment: Write Your Own Restaurant Review

A. Reviewing the reviews
Over a period of two weeks, read whatever restaurant reviews appear in your local newspaper. Note these points in your journal:
1. the name of the restaurant
2. the aspects of the dinner that are discussed
3. whether the review is favorable or unfavorable
4. whether you would like to try the restaurant yourself

B. Writing a review
Pick one of the restaurants that you read about above and eat there yourself. Take note of the same aspects of the dinner that were discussed in the review that you read. Notice where you agree or disagree with the reviewer. Then write a brief essay reviewing the restaurant yourself. Use the original article as a model of how to organize your own review.

Chicago Tribune

SectionSix
Leisure Time

1
Natural selection

2
A party in a basket

Focus on Culture
Leisure Time

Chicago Tribune

Leisure Time

Consumers of Leisure

"How was your weekend?" This question comes up at workplaces all over the United States every Monday morning as people greet each other. It is another way of asking, "How did you spend your leisure time?"

In the United States the way people spend their leisure time is an important part of their identity. Perhaps everybody does nearly the same thing all day in the office or the factory, but leisure time is what makes people distinct and reveals who they are. Some people like rock music, for example, and others may like jazz or classical music. Some people are runners or swimmers, and others are "couch potatoes" who "surf" the television channels with a remote control. Some go to museums while others spend long hours at a mall. These kinds of choices are ways that people define themselves.

It hasn't always been this way. "Leisure time" was almost unknown in the United States in the eighteenth and nineteenth centuries. When most people worked on farms, the workday was from sunrise to sunset every day except Sunday, which was devoted to church. Later, with the rise of factories and city populations, people worked equally long hours and had only Sunday for rest. Some people did many of the things then that they do now—attend concerts, have parties, go to restaurants, read novels, or play sports—but to a much lesser extent.

Slowly, throughout the twentieth century, leisure time grew. Technology made farm work less burdensome, and changes in laws shortened the factory work day and week. New inventions such as the phonograph and the radio gave people access to music and mass entertainment on a scale unknown before. People gradually became consumers of entertainment, and businesses competed aggressively for their dollars.

For many people leisure time means going somewhere—to a museum, to a concert, to a restaurant, or to a baseball game, for example. Or it means doing something such as playing volleyball, backpacking, swimming, biking, singing in a chorus, or playing in a park with their children. For other people free time means staying home with wonderful sources of entertainment, such as a VCR, stereo, or cable TV with dozens of channels. Others pursue creative activities such as cooking, gardening, and home improvement. The latest stay-at-home activity is "surfing the net"—that is, looking for information and entertainment on the Internet.

In the United States, leisure time is big business. Enormous amounts of money are spent by competing enterprises that make and sell the goods and services that people use in their free time. In fact, shopping itself is an important leisure time activity. Spending a day at a giant mall has become, for some people, as interesting as spending the day at a museum or amusement park.

People in the United States are ultimately not much different from others in what they do in their leisure time. The real difference may lie in the energy, time, money, and sheer enthusiasm that they devote to it.

Chicago Tribune

Preparation

Natural selection

Previewing the Article

Surfing is a thrilling and dangerous activity in which a person balances on a board and rides the surface of a big, crashing ocean wave. *Channel surfing,* the subject of this article, is a bit different. In this activity a person sits on a couch and pushes the button of a television remote-control device many times a minute to check and recheck all the channels. In the United States, channel surfing is by far the more popular sport.

When television first replaced radio, in the 1950s, channel surfing was unknown. Back then, there were only a few stations. Viewers had their favorite shows and watched them devotedly all the way through. In fact, studies showed that when a family sat down to watch a favorite program at 7 P.M., they stayed with the same channel the rest of the evening.

With the coming of cable television, dozens of channels now offer a great variety of feature films, situation comedies, news, weather, talk shows, science shows, documentaries, and advertising. Faced with so many choices, viewers often become restless and feel a need to check out all the other stations.

As this article explains, men in a typical U.S. household usually want to hold the remote control and surf the channels; women usually like to choose one program and watch it through.

The following definitions will help you read the article with greater understanding:

- *attention span* is a term that indicates how long a person can concentrate on one activity. A poor attention span may hinder learning. TV has often been accused of weakening viewers' attention spans.
- *Attention Deficit Disorder,* or *ADD,* is a learning problem usually associated with school children, but anyone may have it. A child with ADD has difficulty doing one task, such as reading or writing, for longer than a few minutes.

- *Nielsen Media Research* is the most prominent company that the networks use to compile statistics on television viewing. If Nielsen determines that many viewers watch a particular program, the network can charge advertisers higher amounts to run commercials during the program.

Before You Read

Discuss the following questions:
1. How do you watch TV? Do you watch one show straight through, or do you channel-surf?
2. Do you think there is a difference between the way men and women watch television?
3. Read the headline. What two meanings does the word *selection* have here? What do you know about Darwin's Theory of Natural Selection?
4. Is there a word for *channel surfing* in your native language? Is this a common way to watch television in your culture?

As You Read

As you read, try to answer this question: Who channel-surfs and why?

Rather than
numbing
their brains,
TV channel surfers
may simply
be proving
Darwin's
theory

Natural selection

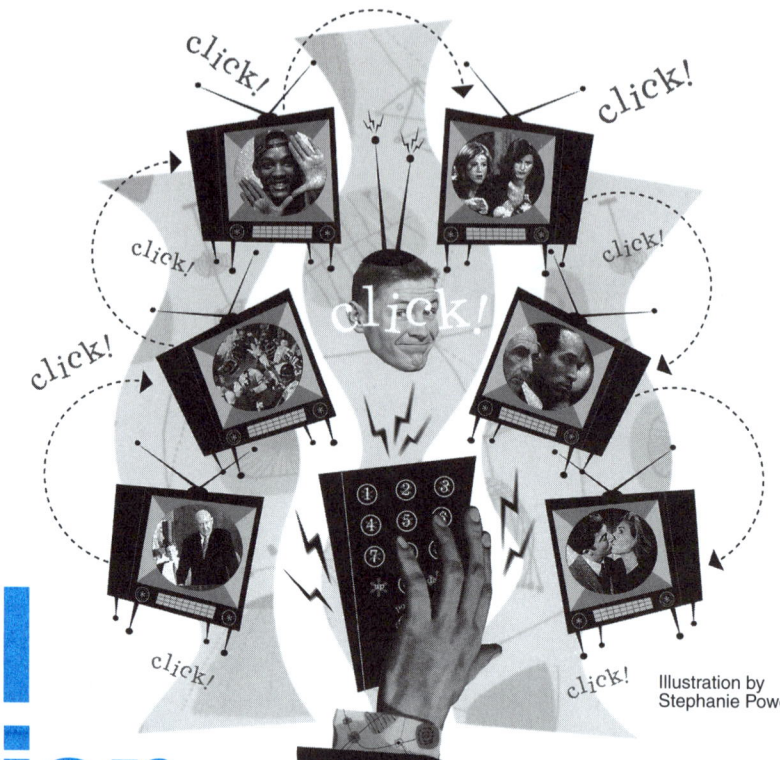

Illustration by
Stephanie Power

By Jon Van
TRIBUNE STAFF WRITER

1   Tim Bauhs watches television more like a traffic cop than a couch potato, often listening to a compact disc and reading a book while using his remote control to flip past channel after channel, seldom pausing.

2   "We get about 50 channels, and the only time I really ever stop on one for any length of time is when the phone rings or something else distracts me," said Bauhs, who lives in Chicago's Wicker Park neighborhood.

3   "Most guys I know in their 20s watch TV this way; it's just for relaxation, you don't really want to watch anything. I surf the Internet the same way with my computer. It's easier to get lost on the Internet and you feel more intelligent surfing there than TV, but really it doesn't make much difference because it's all trash anyway."

4   Bauhs is a bright, busy young man who works as a college administrator and is attending graduate school. He grew up in a home where TV watching was discouraged and has never really spent much time viewing programs from start to finish as many older people do.

5   He could be a poster boy for the frenetic TV viewing habits that can drive wives and girlfriends crazy as well as cause parents to fret that the younger generation is losing its attention span.

6   But Bauhs doesn't see it that way. He finds TV grazing a natural response to the drivel available on most channels most of the time.

7   "This isn't an attention deficit disorder," he said. "It's a thirst for more information, more knowledge. I can easily watch three games at the same time and not miss a thing. If you do miss something, you'll catch the replay."

8   Interestingly, many scholars say Bauhs is probably right. Rather than representing a decline in intellectual ability, channel surfing may more properly be seen as an adaptive strategy for coping with the modern world.

9   "It certainly is a popular theory that TV is destroying young people's attention span," said Bernard Beck, associate professor of sociology at Northwestern University.

"But I don't know of any well-designed research to show that is the case."

10   Another view, said Beck, is that channel surfing helps people to break out of the linear mode of receiving information represented by reading a book. One man's shortened attention span may be another's survival strategy, he said.

11   More and more, people are called upon to switch their attention among many things in their work, which usually involves sitting in front of a computer screen and interacting with it.

12   "Humans are very adaptive," Beck said. "We can transform ourselves into any kind of creature the environment calls for. The person with a limited attention span is also someone who can adapt to a world where business is done on screen and on-line."

13   Just as bear and tiger cubs learn survival skills through their play, humans also use recreation to acquire skills helpful in their work, he said. Today's TV channel surfer may become tomorrow's quintessential computerized deal-maker.

14   Not only is there little evidence that channel surfing destroys attention span, but the popular concept of attention span is too fuzzy to mean much to scholars, said Gordon Logan, a psychology pro-

fessor at the University of Illinois at Urbana-Champaign.

15 "In most studies psychologists do, attention span refers to the amount of information a person absorbs rather than the duration of time spent in the process," Logan said. "The studies are usually concerned with performance, not with whether someone becomes bored.

16 "If people were overwhelmed with the information they get from channel surfing, they wouldn't do it. The person with a TV clicker in his hand, moving through the channels, is happy. When I control the remote, I'm happy, but when my wife does it, she doesn't do it right for me.

17 "This is the leading edge of interactive technology."

18 Although people in the TV industry are aware of channel surfing, they profess to be unconcerned by it, perhaps because they are unsure what else to do.

19 "Senior ad agency decision makers are aware of it, but they think its effect on TV commercials is negligible right now, although it has future prospects of becoming more significant," said Ave Butensky, president of the Television Bureau of Advertising, a trade association for broadcasters.

Counting the clickers

20 People who click non-stop through an array of TV channels don't get counted as viewing any one program for ratings purposes, which are what dictate the amount advertisers pay to air commercials.

21 Anne Elliot, a spokeswoman for Nielsen Media Research, said that a viewer being tracked by Nielsen must watch a program for several minutes without changing channels for it to register in the ratings.

22 Devices installed by Nielsen to monitor viewer habits could register the many channel changes caused by TV grazing, she said, but that information isn't part of the general ratings. Clients could pay to get such detailed information, she said.

23 Oddly, changing from one channel to another often may not result in a viewer's getting significantly different information.

24 In his book about the media, *A Mathematician Reads the Newspaper* (Basic Books), John Allen Paulos noted that when he switches from one network news show to another, he often finds they are reporting on the same story.

25 Paulos, a mathematics professor at Temple University, calculated that if there are five or six major stories of the day and each station presents them in random order, there is a 63 percent chance that two stations will be running their reports on the same topic at the same time.

26 But because stations don't present news stories in random order, the chances of seeing the same story on different channels at the same time is even greater than 63 percent, Paulos wrote.

27 In a general way, the same notion spills over to most entertainment programs too, said Arno Penzias, vice president for research at AT&T Bell Laboratories.

28 "In the case of TV sitcoms or adventure shows, you have very little diversity," said Penzias, a Nobel Prize winner in physics. "There are only so many ways you can have people meeting half-nude in a bathroom making salacious wisecracks, only so many ways to show automobiles chasing each other through cities and only so many ways to photograph a helicopter exploding in mid-air.

29 "So people who have seen these things several times before will tend to get bored upon seeing them once again and will switch to another channel where other scenes they have seen before are being replayed."

30 TV channel grazing is just one aspect of the modern world in which the trend is to offer consumers tremendous choice with very low transaction costs.

31 "There is a man who now offers customers their choice from among 500 mutual funds," said Penzias. "You can buy and sell these funds as often as you want, by pushing buttons on a computer. You can get in and out of the market as effortlessly as changing TV channels."

32 As long as television continues to offer commodity fare, more people will become bored with it and adopt the surfing approach to their viewing, Penzias predicted.

33 "Today, with such an abundance of information and people all being so busy, the scarcest thing you'll find is someone's full attention," he said. "That's what is driving the information industry right now." A guy thing.

34 Of course, even a devoted clicker-flipper like Tim Bauhs acknowledges that it isn't for everyone.

35 "Women don't really get into channel surfing like guys do," he said. "In fact, just about the only time I watch a show clear through is when I'm watching with a woman."

36 Another devoted channel flipper, Charley Cook, who shares a Gold Coast apartment with his fiancee, echoes that sentiment. "Among men, only the Amish will watch one show at a time," he joked.

37 But his fiancee can't track shows with Cook's speed, he said.

38 "I can tell instantly if I want to see more of a show, and if I don't, I'll move on, but she'll say, 'What was that?' and ask me to flip back," he said. "Usually I control the remote."

39 Claire Laible, Cook's fiancee, said that when she does have the remote control, she rarely uses it to switch channels during shows she is watching.

40 When Cook starts flipping from one channel to the next, "it makes me nuts," she said. "I usually go into the next room and watch a different TV or read a book."

41 The growing gap between men and women in TV viewing habits was a major theme used by comedian Rob Becker in his one-man show, "Defending the Caveman."

42 Men, Becker contends, are by nature hunters who keenly focus upon one thing at a time. They switch through TV channels seeking that one thing upon which to focus while women are by nature gatherers who want to spend time to take in everything around them.

43 Man's appetite for channel surfing is probably limited right now by technology, said Logan, the U. of I. psychologist.

44 "The company that brings out a set allowing you to watch four channels at once would enjoy brisk sales," he says, "if only they could sort out the problem of separating the sound from all those channels."

Chicago Tribune
Postreading

I. Getting the Message

After reading the article, choose the best answer for each item.

1. This article is mainly about
   a. how television is bad for one's mental health.
   b. the ways people watch television.
   c. new television technology.
2. The experts interviewed about channel surfing think that
   a. TV viewing habits are getting worse.
   b. TV viewing habits are very interesting.
   c. TV viewing habits have not changed in 50 years.
3. According to the article, women
   a. like to channel-surf.
   b. do not understand why men channel-surf.
   c. do not like television.
4. According to the article, men in their twenties
   a. probably channel-surf more than older men.
   b. probably channel-surf to find the best shows to watch.
   c. probably channel-surf less than women in their twenties.
5. An important idea of the article is that channel surfing is probably
   a. a natural response to changing technology.
   b. a problem that requires the attention of psychologists.
   c. a bad way to watch television.

Check your answers with the key on page 165. If you have made mistakes, reread the article to gain a better understanding of it.

II. Expanding Your Vocabulary

A. Getting Meaning from Context

Find each word or phrase in the paragraph indicated in parentheses. Use context clues to determine the meaning of the word or phrase. Choose the best definition.

1. frenetic (5)   a. slow   b. overexcited
2. drivel (6)   a. worthwhile material   b. worthless material
3. decline (8)   a. decrease in value   b. strange growth
4. quintessential (13)   a. necessary   b. perfect
5. negligible (19)   a. slight or small   b. neglected, unused
6. salacious (28)   a. intelligent   b. improper
7. scarcest (33)   a. hardest to find   b. most common
8. brisk (44)   a. fast, active   b. weak

Chicago Tribune

Postreading

B. Defining Verbs from the Article

Match each phrase on the left with the one on the right that has the same meaning. For context clues reread the paragraphs indicated in parentheses.

1. To flip (1) past something means	a. to get it.
2. To switch (11) something means	b. to determine it .
3. To acquire (13) something means	c. to record it.
4. To profess (18) something means	d. to claim it.
5. To dictate (20) something means	e. to change to something else.
6. To register (21) something means	f. to repeat it.
7. To acknowledge (34) something means	g. to say you believe it.
8. To echo (36) means	h. to go very quickly.
9. To contend (42) something means	i. to admit it.

III. Working with Idioms and Expressions

Study the meanings of the idioms and expressions below. A form of each one appears in the paragraph indicated in parentheses.

couch potato (1) a person who spends many hours sitting watching TV

surf the Internet (3) rapidly check what is available on the Internet with a computer

make much difference (3) create a significant difference, matter

see it that way (6) agree

catch the replay (7) see the videotaped replay of a play in a game

linear mode (10) the idea that, when any information is presented, the first thing must be understood before the second thing, the second before the third, and so on

called upon (11) asked to do something

calls for (12) demands, requires

on-line (12) connected to the Internet

spills over (27) is connected to

get into (35) become interested in

take in (42) see, know about

bring out (44) produce and sell

sort out (44) solve

Complete the sentences below using the idioms and expressions.

1. A physically fit, athletic person doesn't want to be considered a _____ .

2. Computer companies _____ new computers and computer programs so fast that few people consider themselves knowledgeable about new technology.

3. It seems that most women do not _____ channel surfing the way men do.

4. Some men are not interested in watching a basketball game all the way through because they know that they can _____ later.

Chicago Tribune

Postreading

IV. Focusing on Style and Tone

Objective Tone in a Feature Story

Like a news article, this feature story seems very objective in its tone because the writer so seldom expresses his own opinion. The writer's opinion is revealed mainly in his choice of people interviewed. Two kinds of people were interviewed: experts, such as scientists and business people, and nonexperts—in this case, people who can be considered representative of the cultural trend. Their ideas are presented in two ways:

- **quotations:** the writer uses the exact words that a person spoke or wrote, in quotation marks.
- **paraphrase:** the writer restates someone's idea in different words, without quotation marks.

In this exercise read the paragraph indicated in the left column and answer these questions:

Who was interviewed? Is the person an expert or a nonexpert (E or N)? Are the person's words quoted or paraphrased (Q or P)?

	Paragraph	Person Interviewed	E or N	Q or P
1.	2			
2.	10			
3.	19			
4.	26			
5.	31			
6.	40			

V. Talking and Writing

Discuss the topics below. Then choose one of them to write about.

1. One of the channel surfers in this article, Tim Bauhs, says that channel surfing comes from a "thirst for more information." Do you think this is true? If you channel-surf, are you searching for more information?

2. Many people in the United States fear that television is bad for children. People think it reduces children's attention span and hinders their ability do school work. Is this an issue in your native country?

3. Two of those interviewed in this article say that television has very poor content. What do you think? Can watching television be a good use of your time?

Chicago Tribune

Preparation

A party in a basket

Previewing the Article

Although people in the United States spend a great deal of time at their jobs, many are often preoccupied with children at the same time. In fact, U.S. parents have a tendency to spoil their children by giving them a great deal of gifts. Often, these gifts are a substitute for the attention that people are too busy to give their children. This situation naturally presents a problem for parents torn between work and the desire to shower as much love and affection as possible on their youngsters. However, almost anything in the United States can be packaged and sold, and for almost every need there is an eager *entrepreneur* interested in making a sale. So parents' needs inevitably lead to the creation of new businesses.

"A Tisket a Tasket, A Party in a Basket" is the creative name of a business that helps parents plan their children's birthday parties. These days, many parents have little time to plan a party themselves since both parents in a household typically work full-time. When they *are* free, they spend much of their time driving children to a wide variety of after-school activities—because the children are busy too.

However, giving a child an entertaining birthday party has great importance for many parents. So even something as simple as a birthday party can be planned and put together by a business. In addition to "A Tisket a Tasket" there are actually a large number of businesses that exist solely to serve children's birthday parties: party stores, toy stores, clowns, magicians, bands, and decorators are all sources that, for a price, parents can turn to for help with a birthday celebration.

Before You Read

Discuss the following questions:
1. Describe a typical children's birthday party in your native country. What games are played? What do the children eat and drink? What songs are sung? What kinds of gifts are given? What other customs are followed?
2. Have you ever been to a child's birthday party in the United States? Did anything about the party surprise you? Describe the event.

As You Read

Try to imagine the size of the party basket described in the article. What hints does the article give about its size?

A party in a
basket

Beth Anaclerio (left) and Jill Carlisle started their own home party planning business last year.
Tribune photo by Jose More.

By Julie Morse

1   A child's birthday party doesn't have to be a hassle to be a barrel—or basket—of fun, according to Beth Anaclerio, an Evanston mother of two, ages 4 and 18 months.

2   "Having a party at home usually requires a lot of running around on the part of the parent, and often the birthday boy or girl gets lost in the frenzy. But it really doesn't have to be that way," said Anaclerio. Last summer, Anaclerio and her friend Jill Carlisle, a Northbrook mother of a 4- and 2-year-old, founded a home party-planning business called "A Tisket a Tasket, a Party in a Basket." Their goal is to help parents and children share in the fun part of party planning, like choosing the theme or making a cake, while they handle all the time-consuming details.

3   Drawing on their experiences as mothers and former buyers for Marshall Field's, they have created 10 ready-to-use, home party packages. Everything a family needs to plan and host a memorable party, except the cake and ice cream, is delivered to the home in a large basket.

4   "Our parties are geared for children 2 to 10," Anaclerio said, "and they're very interactive and creative in that they build a sense of drama based on a theme. For example, at the Soda Shoppe party the guests become waiters and waitresses and build wonderful ice cream creations."

5   The standard $200 package for eight children includes a basket brimming with invitations, personalized keepsakes, craft kits, games and prizes, a centerpiece, paper goods and a party planner. For more information, call Anaclerio at 708-864-6584 or Carlisle at 708-205-9141.

Chicago Tribune

Postreading

I. Getting the Message

After reading the article, choose the best answer for each item.

1. The business described in the article
   a. was created by two mothers.
   b. is a large corporation.
   c. has been successful for many years.

2. "A Tisket a Tasket, a Party in a Basket"
   a. does all the planning for a birthday party.
   b. encourages the parents and children to help plan the party.
   c. creates a theme for the party and leaves the details to the parents.

3. The creators of the business were once
   a. entertainers.
   b. home decorators.
   c. buyers for a store.

4. An important idea behind the party planning is that
   a. the children actively participate.
   b. the children sit and watch good entertainers.
   c. the children relax and the parents take care of everything.

5. Because the party basket contains invitations, we can conclude that
   a. the basket is delivered on the day of the party.
   b. the basket is delivered during the party.
   c. the basket is delivered before the party.

Check your answers with the key on page 165. If you have made mistakes, reread the article to gain a better understanding of it.

II. Expanding Your Vocabulary

A. Getting Meaning from Context

Find each word in the paragraph indicated in parentheses. Use context clues to determine the meaning of the word. Choose the best definition.

1. frenzy (2)   a. state of depression   b. state of excitement
2. founded (2)   a. made, established   b. discovered by accident
3. former (3)   a. in an earlier time   b. in a later time
4. theme (4)   a. music   b. main idea
5. creations (4)   a. something made   b. something that is useful
                          with imagination
6. package (5)   a. a set sold as a single item b. box
7. keepsakes (5)   a. private things   b. small gifts
8. centerpiece (5)   a. a decoration for the   b. a small part of a
                          middle of a table   central area

Chicago Tribune

Postreading

B. Using Word Forms

In this article a form of the word *create* is used as a verb, *have created* (paragraph 3); as an adjective, *creative* (paragraph 4); and as a noun, *creation* (paragraph 4). Write the verb and noun forms of the following adjectives used in the article. Use a dictionary if necessary.

		Verb	Noun
1.	memorable		
2.	interactive		
3.	personalized		

Now write the adjective and noun forms of the following verbs used in the article.

		Adjective	Noun
1.	require		
2.	include		

III. Working with Idioms and Expressions

Study the meanings of the idioms and expressions below. A form of each one appears in the paragraph indicated in parentheses.

a hassle (1) a struggle
a barrel of fun (1) a lot of fun
running around (2) going on short trips
"A tisket, a tasket . . . " (2) from a children's nursery rhyme. The first lines are
"A tisket, a tasket, a green and yellow basket. I wrote a letter to my friend, and on the way I lost it."
time-consuming (2) using up or taking a lot of time
ready-to-use (3) prepared ahead of time
geared for (4) made specifically and intended for
sense of drama (4) feeling of excitement
brimming with (5) full of, having an abundance of

Now answer the following questions:
1. Why is preparing a child's birthday party *a hassle* for many parents?
2. When parents do a lot of *running around* before a party, where do they go?
3. Besides the party-in-a-basket idea, what other common *ready-to-use* things can you think of?
4. If a party basket were *geared for* an adult birthday party, what sorts of things would it contain?

Chicago Tribune

Postreading

IV. Making Sense of Sentences

Most writers and speakers, most of the time, use the active voice, in which the performer of an action is the subject of the verb.

Example: Many people read the newspaper every day. (The subject of the verb, *people*, is the doer of the action, *read*.)

Writers and speakers also use the passive voice, in which the subject of the verb is the object of an action and the performer of the action is missing or indicated in a prepositional phrase.

Example: The newspaper is read every day.

The subject of the verb, *newspaper*, is the object of an action. The doer of the action, *people*, is obvious and eliminated.

The article contains two examples of the passive voice. Rewrite each sentence in the active voice and supply the missing performer of the action.

1. (paragraph 3) "Everything a family needs to plan and host a memorable party, except the cake and ice cream, is delivered to the home in a large basket." _____

   _____

   _____

2. (paragraph 4) "'Our parties are geared for children 2 to 10,' Anaclerio said." _____

   _____

   _____

V. Talking and Writing

Discuss the topics below. Then choose one of them to write about.
   1. Would there be a need for this kind of party service in your native country? Why or why not?
   2. Only one party theme is mentioned in the article, the "Soda Shoppe." What other "party themes" can you think of for children? Have you ever gone to an adult party with a theme?
   3. The basic party in a basket service costs $200. Many people in the United States spend this much and more for a child's birthday party. Does this seem excessive to you? Why or why not?

Chicago Tribune

Focus on Culture

Setting the Scene

Leisure time in the United States is serious business. And newspapers strongly reflect this fact. Nearly every sort of leisure activity appears in some form or other in the newspaper, either as advertising, in review articles, in interviews and feature stories, or as straight information about what's happening in the area. The newspaper is probably the most valued source of information about entertainment, for most people want to know something about what they plan to do or where they plan to go before they spend money.

The newspaper is also an entertainment source in itself, and reading it is a favorite leisure activity for many. A common Sunday morning scene, for example, is that of the family spread out in the living room with various sections of the big Sunday edition in each person's hands or on the floor. Many people spend many happy hours each week reading the newspaper.

Information about leisure-time activities can be found in many areas of the newspaper.

- **Features Section.** On an average weekday, most entertainment stories and advertisements are in this section. In large newspapers in big cities, however, various kinds of leisure activities appear in separate sections on the weekend. Most television reviews and feature stories appear in this section.
- **Weekend Activities Section.** In the *Chicago Tribune* this section is called "Friday," and in other newspapers it is called by other names. The *Tribune*'s section contains extensive information about all the music concerts, stage plays, films, dance concerts, restaurants, and special events in the city, such as neighborhood art fairs and fund-raisers. It gives prices, times, location, and sometimes a summary of the content of the event.
- **Movie Section.** Most large newspapers contain a separate movie review section appearing on Friday or Sunday. Readers turn to this section to find what their favorite reviewers are saying about the latest films, which usually open on Friday each week.
- **Book Review Section.** Appearing in most newspapers on Sunday, the book review is more than just a source of opinion about the latest books. It is also a source of lively essays written by experts on the subjects of the books that they are discussing. The book review section also contains a weekly bestseller list and news about readings and book signings by authors.
- **Travel Section.** This section contains many ads and feature stories about travel and vacations. Frequently, these articles also have valuable information about prices, hotels, weather, and other aspects of travel.

Chicago Tribune

Focus on Culture

Here are some of the kinds of articles that can be found in the Friday and Sunday editions of American newspapers that deal with popular leisure-time activities.

Reviews	**Feature Stories**	**News Stories and Information**
a novel	travel article	a neighborhood event
a nonfiction book	article about an author	a stage play
a rock concert	story about a concert	information about a play
a TV show	story about a film	story about a neighborhood event
a classical concert	architecture	a future concert
an art exhibit	a movie star	the entertainment industry
a movie	an author	interview with an actor or director

In addition, look for advertisements for novels, movies, and amusement parks.

Exercise 1. Journal Assignment: Culture Comparison

For two weeks scan your local newspaper for the kinds of stories listed above. Complete the chart by answering the following questions: 1. What is the headline? 2. What kind of article is it? 3. Was the article interesting to you? (Yes or No) 4. Would this kind of article appear in a newspaper in your native country? (Yes or No)

	Headline	Kind	Interesting?	In Your Native Country?
1.				
2.				
3.				
4.				
5.				
6.				

Chicago Tribune

Focus on Culture

Exercise 2. Reading a Movie Ad

Find a movie ad that appeals to you and that makes a movie seem like one you would like to see. Answer these questions about the ad.

1. What is the title of the film?
2. Who is the director?
3. Who are the major actors?
4. How big is the ad? Is it bigger than other ads or the same size?
5. Describe the picture in the ad. What is appealing about it?
6. What favorable quotations (called "blurbs") from reviewers appear in the ad? What newspapers, magazines, or other media sources are they from?
7. Why do you think that you would like to see this film?

Exercise 3. Review the Reviewers

On the day a film opens in your area, find two reviews of it from separate newspapers (you may have to go to a library to do this). After you have read the reviews, see the film as soon as you can.

Which reviewer's reaction to the film is closer to your own? Write an essay comparing the two reviews. Be sure to include such details as the reviewers' opinions of the film's plot, characters, script, direction, and acting.

Exercise 4. Understanding the Special Vocabulary of Reviews

Some of the art forms less common than television and film that are reviewed in newspapers are the following:

operas	dance concerts	museum exhibitions
performance art	bluegrass	comedians
art exhibits	classical concerts	jazz concerts

Find one review from the list above and write down five terms used in the review that are unfamiliar to you. Look them up in a good dictionary, write their definitions, and use each in a sentence.

Exercise 5. Take a Dream Vacation

Newspaper travel sections contain wonderful feature stories about places to visit. Imagine that you have all the money you would need for any trip at all. Then look over several issues of travel sections and find an article about an especially beautiful or interesting spot. Answer the following questions about the article:

1. What place does the article discuss?
2. What are two of the special features of the place according to the author?
3. Why does this place appeal to you?
4. What would you do on this vacation?

Chicago Tribune

Religion

1

Xers finding faith their destination

2

Church singles groups find way to loosen up, keep faith

3

Religious groups push campaign fund reforms

Focus on Culture

Religion

Religion

A Compromise Between Two Values

Two famous sentences summarize the role of religion in the cultural life of the United States. The first is from Article 1 of the Bill of Rights: "Congress shall make no law respecting an establishment of religion, or prohibiting the free exercise thereof." The second appears on every penny: "In God we trust."

Both these statements reveal the significance of religion in the United States, but they also reveal a conflict between opposing ideals. The first asserts the separation of church and state. In fact, one of the main reasons early immigrants from Europe came to America was to practice their religions without government interference. The Pilgrims, for example, were called *Separatists* because they wanted to separate from the Church of England, a state church.

Originally, each colonial area of the Atlantic coast was largely settled according to religious affiliation: Congregationalists in New England, members of the Church of England in the South, and a mixture of Baptists and Quakers in the Middle Atlantic region. When the United States was formed, the writers, called *framers*, of the new Constitution wanted to ensure that all citizens could practice their various religions freely, without government interference. So protection of religious diversity, along with the cultural diversity that underlies it, was written into the Constitution.

The other statement—"In God we trust"—also attests to the importance of religion in the United States but seems to run counter to the idea of separation of church and state. Stamped on the penny at the request of Abraham Lincoln, this saying is almost a national statement of faith. And religion comes up even at the inauguration of the president, at which a prayer is said and the president takes his oath of office with a hand placed on a Bible.

The two values of cultural diversity and a common culture can come into conflict. For example, some people, fearing that the separation of church and state leads to a godless society, advocate an amendment to the Constitution that would permit prayer in public schools. Other people oppose this idea and see it as a sly form of state-sponsored religion. But despite these disagreements, people in the United States live with a compromise between these two values, and this in itself is something of a triumph in a world in which many countries are shaken by religious wars.

Chicago Tribune

Preparation

Xers finding faith their destination

Previewing the Article

Do you know what a *generation gap* is? This term indicates an important and sometimes difficult feature of family life in the United States. People are accustomed to thinking that there will always be a big difference between the values of parents and their grown-up children. This difference—this gap between the generations—is sometimes dramatic. For example, after World War II the children of the soldiers who returned from the war were called *Baby Boomers*. This generation rejected the music, the clothing, the lifestyle, and many of the values of their parents and strongly opposed U.S. involvement in the Vietnam War.

Now these baby boomers have grown-up children who are often referred to as *Generation Xers*. The *X* in the name reflects the commonly held idea that these young adults—who are mostly in their twenties—have no name and therefore no clear identity, lifestyle, or culture of their own. However, as the article points out, the young people of Generation X are much more serious and spiritual than the older generation understands. Not only are Generation Xers attending church in greater numbers, but they are enthusiastically embracing older, more traditional religions as well.

Before You Read

Before you read the article, discuss the following questions:

1. This article mentions three religions with historic traditions: Roman Catholicism, Judaism, and Eastern Orthodoxy. How old are these faiths?
2. Can you think of other religions with ancient roots? What religions have long histories in your native country?
3. Discuss the meanings of these words related to the use of computers: *Internet, World Wide Web, E-mail, web site, cyberstudents, chat room.*

As You Read

1. This article contrasts negative and positive ideas about a generation of Americans. What negative words are used to describe them? What one positive word is used?
2. As you read this article, think about the generation gap in the United States and compare this situation with the way different generations see each other in your native country.

Xers finding faith their destination

Generation returning to religions steeped in tradition, spirituality

By Cathleen Falsani
<small>TRIBUNE STAFF WRITER</small>

1   They've been called slackers and Xers, the legion of listless twentysomethings who shuffle their directionless way from one coffeehouse to another, nary a goal in mind. They are accused of apathy, disconnection and an inability to commit—even four years at the same college is for many a daunting leap of faith.

2   But if the crowds of young adults who have warmed the pews of many churches and synagogues in recent years are any indication, the lost generation may have found religion.

3   "We are looking for something that's not vapid or temporary," said Jeremy Langford, a 26-year-old Catholic and a managing editor at Loyola University Press in Chicago.

Young people (above) can be found in ever greater numbers among the congregation at Holy Transfiguration Antiochian Orthodox Church in Wheaton, where Rev. Bill Caldaroni (top) leads evening vespers.
<small>Tribune photos by Ed Wagner.</small>

4   "I'm looking for someone who will take me by the hand and say, 'Why don't you walk with me awhile and I'll take you to the mountain top and show you the view,'" said Langford, who edited *This Man Bernardin*. "Seekers" is a more fitting description for his generation, Langford said.

5   Rev. Bill Caldaroni, 41, pastor of Holy Transfiguration Antiochian Orthodox Church in Wheaton, agreed.

6   "They have a thirst for worship and spirituality . . . mystical things that are not so much cerebral," Caldaroni said.

7   Since 1993, two dozen students from nearby Wheaton College have joined Caldaroni's parish, making a change from evangelical Protestantism to Eastern Orthodoxy. It's a scenario not particular to Orthodoxy, Caldaroni said. "There is a sense of despair in that whole generation," he said. Many young adults find comfort in practices that have old traditions and long histories, like Judaism, Eastern Orthodoxy and Roman Catholicism, he said. "Those (traditions) are something rooted," he said. "They need that."

8   Roman Catholicism, Eastern Orthodoxy and Judaism have all experienced an increased involvement of people in their 20s and 30s over the last five years, according to religious leaders.

9   "They really feel somehow cheated, that some of the past has been taken away from them," said Rabbi Sheldon Zimmerman, president of Hebrew Union College, which has campuses in Cincinnati, Los Angeles and New York.

10   The oldest existing rabbinical seminary in the country, Hebrew Union College is adapting its methods for training rabbis and Jewish laity to meet the changing demands of its students.

11   Among the innovations is a class offered exclusively over the Internet. A professor posts his lecture, readings and an assignment for cyberstudents across the country. They E-mail him back with their answers and comments. "By using (the Internet), we can do things that enable people to connect and find their way," Zimmerman said. In addition to the Internet course offerings, by next year, nearly a third of the college's library holdings will be available on a web site.

12   Some clergy, who have realized that many members of the "Sesame Street" generation are more comfortable in an Internet chat room than a church sanctuary, have embraced the World Wide Web as a means of outreach and discipleship.

13   Via E-mail, Rev. John Matusiak, pastor of St. Joseph Orthodox Church in Wheaton, shepherded a university student in Scotland through his chrismation, an Orthodox rite akin to confirmation. Matusiak even flew to the Polish monastery where the Scottish student's chrismation took place earlier this year.

14   Matusiak's parish has grown exponentially in recent years, mostly due to the addition of Gen-Xers and thirtysomethings, many of whom have started families and want to put down roots.

15   "They have a real thirst for some sort of permanence," he said.

16   "They don't have their own youth culture. We've raised a whole group of children who have appropriated their parent's culture," said the 46-year-old Matusiak, who added that his college-age children listen to Janis Joplin and wear tie-dyed clothes, fixtures from his own college days.

17   "(Religion) gives some kind of stability in a culture where they don't know what is lasting and what is permanent," he said.

18   "The backbone of many parishes used to be 25- to 30-year-olds, the same group that people now are wringing their hands over and saying, 'Where are they?'" said Rev. John Cusick, head of young adult ministries for the Catholic Archdiocese of Chicago.

19   "They haven't left. They haven't gone anywhere," Cusick said. "Everybody is talking about a spiritual hunger in younger Americans. They're having a hard time getting that hunger fed."

20   Young adults who have found traditional religious paradigms cramped are exploring innovative ways to express their faith and religious beliefs.

21   Hillel, the leading national Jewish campus ministry, recognized this and in 1993 created a team of recent college graduates called the Jewish Campus Service Corps, to reach the traditionally unreachable students.

22   One-year Service Corps fellows infiltrate elusive Jewish social groups, such as sororities and fraternities, and try to involve the students in Jewish activities.

23   At Northwestern University three years ago, the Corps fellows began hosting a Friday night Shabbat meal in one of the Greek houses. Now many Jewish sorority and fraternity members are active in volunteer projects.

24   "We don't want them to be Jewish on our terms—we want them to be Jewish on their terms," said Julie Lyss, 29, the assistant director of The Hillels of Illinois.

25   Lyss is a typical seeker: After graduating from a women's college with a degree in communications, she made a conscious decision to invest her time in her own faith community.

26   "I feel that it is an absolute expression of my Jewishness," she said. "Clearly this is something I am passionate about or I wouldn't be making half the money I could be making."

Chicago Tribune

Postreading

I. Getting the Message

After reading the article, choose the best answer for each item.

1. This article is mainly about
   a. how young adults are turning to religion.
   b. how young adults are kept away from traditional churches.
   c. how young adults are receiving great attention from newspapers and television.

2. Generation Xers are especially attracted by
   a. new, experimental religions.
   b. traditional, older religions.
   c. academic, intellectual religions.

3. An interesting innovation in religious education has been the use of
   a. television classes.
   b. the Internet.
   c. large lecture courses.

4. "Generation Xers" are usually considered to be
   a. enthusiastic.
   b. aggressive.
   c. lazy.

5. The writer of this article develops the main idea principally by
   a. using statistics from public opinion polls.
   b. quoting religious leaders.
   c. talking personally to large numbers of Xers.

6. The religious leaders interviewed in this article think that
   a. young adults are very interested in spiritual things.
   b. young adults are disappointed in traditional religions.
   c. only college-educated young adults are interested in joining a church.

7. The writer thinks that readers would be surprised to know that
   a. Generation Xers are more complicated and spiritual than most people think.
   b. Generation Xers are neither complicated nor interesting.
   c. Generation Xers are not as interested in religion as their parents' generation.

Check your answers with the key on page 165. If you have made mistakes, reread the article to gain a better understanding of it.

II. Expanding Your Vocabulary

A. Getting Meaning from Context

Use context clues to determine the meaning of each word or phrase found in the paragraphs indicated in parentheses. Choose the correct definition.

1. shuffle (1)   a. hurry   b. walk slowly and uncertainly
2. apathy (1)   a. lack of interest   b. sympathy
3. pews (2)   a. colorful windows   b. benches for sitting in a church
4. vapid (3)   a. dull, not lively   b. full
5. scenario (7)   a. course of action   b. belief
6. exclusively (11)   a. expensively   b. only
7. shepherded (13)   a. guided   b. followed
8. innovative (20)   a. new and creative   b. strange
9. paradigms (20)   a. churches   b. systems of belief

Postreading

B. Reading for Suggested Meanings

Answer the following questions:

1. Why does one man in the article say that the experience of religious insight is like being taken to a *mountain top* (4) and shown the view?

2. What does it mean for a plant to *put down roots* (14)? How can a person do something similar?

3. What are the feelings of people who are *wringing their hands over* (18) the 25- to 30-year-olds in their churches?

III. Analyzing Sentences

Reread the sentences indicated in parentheses and choose the best answer.

1. "They've been called slackers and Xers, the legion of listless twentysomethings who shuffle their directionless way from one coffeehouse to another, nary a goal in mind" (paragraph 1). This sentence presents a picture of
   a. large numbers of active young people having fun.
   b. large numbers of impolite young people drinking coffee.
   c. many lazy young adults walking slowly from one place to another with no purpose in mind.

2. "They are accused of apathy, disconnection and an inability to commit—even four years at the same college is for many a daunting leap of faith" (paragraph 1). Those who accuse the Xers of being unable to set goals are probably
   a. the older generation
   b. religious leaders
   c. young people

3. "'They really feel somehow cheated, that some of the past has been taken away from them,' said Rabbi Sheldon Zimmermann" (paragraph 9). The young adults probably feel cheated because
   a. their parents did not raise them as active members of a traditional religion.
   b. most religions today do not emphasize old traditions.
   c. young adults refuse to study the history of religion.

4. "'We've raised a whole group of children who have appropriated their parent's culture,' said the 46-year-old Matusiak, who added that his college-age children listen to Janis Joplin and wear tie-dyed clothes, fixtures from his own college days" (paragraph 16). The speaker here thinks that
   a. it is unfortunate that young people have the same culture as their parents.
   b. young people are lucky to have the same style of clothes and music as their parents.
   c. having the same culture as their parents provides young people with a satisfying religious life.

Chicago Tribune

Postreading

IV. Talking and Writing

Discuss the topics below. Then choose one of them to write about.

1. Do young adults in your native country usually have the same values and lifestyle as their parents? If they do, what specific things do they have in common? If they do not, how do the young people differ from their parents?

2. How important is religion in your native country? How many different religions are there?

3. Is there a generation gap in the United States (or in the country where you are living) between young people from your native country and their parents? If so, what kinds of differences do you see?

4. Do people "choose" a religious faith in your native country, or are they usually born into one?

5. Do you know any young adults from the United States? Do they attend religious services? Do they ever discuss religion? If so, what do they say about it? How do their attitudes differ from yours?

Chicago Tribune

Preparation

Church singles groups find way to loosen up, keep faith

Previewing the Article

As we all know, people go to church to pray, to meditate, and to worship with others. There are some clergy in Chicago, however, who are trying to add another reason to this list: to have fun.

These clergy know that a church is more than a group of people who pray together. It is a *subculture,* that is, a smaller group with a shared way of life within the larger culture, or society. For this group to maintain its identity and stay attractive to its members, it ought to be a friendly little society of people who know each other in a variety of roles: as co-workers, as friends, and even as partygoers.

All religions hold basic moral values and spiritual beliefs that are different from those of the *secular,* or nonreligious, culture. Thus, they see members pulled away by the attractions of the world outside the church. As this article vividly notes, young adults "historically are disaffected by organized religion" and so are a special challenge for religious leaders attempting to maintain the church's subculture.

The following information will help your understanding of the article:

- The *Arch Deluxe* is a special hamburger sold by McDonald's.
- *Old Town* is an area on Chicago's North Side.
- *The Blackhawks* are the professional hockey team of the National Hockey League in Chicago.
- The film, *The Rocky Horror Picture Show* (1975), is a musical satire of horror movies that is extremely popular with college students and young adults.
- *The Rules: Time-Tested Secrets for Capturing the Heart of Mr. Right* (1996), by Ellen Fein and Sherrie Schneider, is a book that gives advice to young women on how to find a good husband—an ideal man referred to by the authors as "Mr. Right."

Before You Read

Discuss the following questions:

1. Do you belong to a church or religious singles group? What kinds of activities does the group engage in?
2. Do you or does someone you know belong to a religion that forbids certain types of recreation? What is forbidden? Why?
3. Have you or someone you know stopped being an active member of a church? Why? Would a change in the church bring you back as an active member?

As You Read

Count the number of church groups mentioned. How many different religious faiths are represented by these groups?

Church
singles groups
find way to loosen up, keep faith

St. Michael's Social Club members Suzanne Voce (from left), Christina Tavares and Frank Tucker socialize during a recent gathering at Alumni Club Bar & Grill.
Tribune photo by Val Mazzenga.

By Flynn McRoberts
TRIBUNE STAFF WRITER

1   Filing into a recent Sunday evening mass at St. Michael's Catholic Church in Old Town, parishioners were handed the usual hymnal and missal along with a flier from the church social club seeking volunteers to help rebuild a South Side mission.

2   The flier made another pitch as well: dinner for new club members at the Texas Star Fajita Bar after mass.

3   Not exactly the sort of thing you might expect along with your Sunday sermon and solemnity. But it's just one example of the effort by religious groups to help young adults develop their spiritual lives while enjoying, not just enduring, being single.

4   It is happening at a time when churches are realizing they must nurture young adults, who historically are disaffected by organized religion.

5   Competing with a popular culture that often glorifies sexual behavior and hedonistic living scarcely in keeping with most religious tenets, the groups seek to demonstrate that being religious and single is not a gloomy, burdensome existence but actually can be fun.

6   So it is that church singles groups may be found discussing the Christian perspective on *The Rules*—the nationally best-selling book on "Capturing the Heart of Mr. Right"—or gathering at watering holes in a way that gives new meaning to images of "the bar scene."

7   Recognizing that fire-and-brimstone preaching drives off many young people, a growing number of clergy who lead young congregations are eschewing finger-wagging while still trying to buttress the values of their faith.

8   "We figure all the people here are adults and they make adult

choices in their lives," said Rev. Ken Sedlak, an associate pastor at St. Michael's, where the 7 P.M. mass on Sunday is regularly packed with young singles and couples. "What we try to do is deal with the spirituality of people, the personal experience of making Christian values their own."

9 Increasingly, religious leaders are acknowledging that young single members of their congregations struggle mightily with temptations of all sorts and need to feel that abiding by church teachings makes them part of a community—not oddballs in the contemporary social scene.

10 Clergy who lead younger flocks say there is no contradiction between the social and sacred. "We don't separate the sacredness out of the human," said Sedlak. "That's the meaning of incarnation, Jesus becoming human. In every human aspect of life you can meet the spiritual and the sacred."

11 At Anshe Emet synagogue on Chicago's North Side, that sense of community is built with such things as kosher cooking classes and a program called Reclaiming Shabbat, in which members of the congregation take turns playing host to the traditional Friday night meal marking the start of the Jewish sabbath.

12 At St. Michael's, the parish social club uses a mix of service and socializing; one recent Saturday they pitched in to repair a mission and then headed off to a Blackhawks game.

13 "A large part of the churchgoing experience is this sense of community. And I don't think that necessarily has to stay within the four walls of the church," said Dante A. Bacani, 30, the new president of St. Michael's Social Club.

14 Granted, he said: "There's not a lot of service involved in a pub crawl. But it ultimately does foster a sense of community among people. And if that in turn leads someone to participate in the charity events . . . then I think we're helping people to fulfill the sense of service (we) should have as Catholics."

15 Besides, noted Christina Tavares, 30, a financial analyst and member of St. Michael's Social Club, "There's nothing in the Catholic Church that says, 'Thou shalt not have a beer.'"

16 Religious groups for young adults have been around for years. But new ones have formed in recent years, and membership has increased in others.

17 Organizers point to a variety of reasons for the renewed interest, from the tendency of many Americans to get married later in life to an increasingly mobile work force that has people switching jobs and cities more often, leaving them searching for social outlets.

18 "Part of the challenge of our generation, where more and more people have careers that take up a lot of time, is feeling connected to something more than our work or our career, wanting to have meaning in our lives," said Rabbi Charles Savenor, 28, assistant rabbi at Anshe Emet synagogue.

19 Young people who are looking to meet others with similar backgrounds don't necessarily have to attend services. The Graduate and Professional division of The Hillels of Illinois, for instance, sponsors events for people age 22 to 30 separate from synagogues.

20 "It's a connection to Judaism, but it's not in a traditional sense," said Karen Farkas, director of the division. "It's not going to a synagogue necessarily. And no one is going to be asking them how they observe or what they do."

21 Susan Pope, 24, also has found an eagerness for a young adults' group at Grace Episcopal Church in Oak Park. Having moved to Oak Park last September, she noted that "it's very difficult to meet people if you're living alone."

22 Even after-church socials can be intimidating. "You end up going for the door because you don't know anybody and it's too intimidating to go into coffee hour alone," she said.

23 So in recent weeks she simply approached people sitting by themselves after services.

24 "Everyone has been thrilled," she said. "Now I want to go because I know that there are going to be people there that I know, and we have interests in common outside of church."

25 Aware of some criticism, the groups are seeking to change the perception that they are merely places to get dates. To do so, they are expanding their range of activities to also attract older parishioners—and not just singles.

26 The St. Michael's club decided last year to change its name from the Young Adults Group to the Social Club. "We wanted to get away from the belief that this was just a way to get drunk and pick up members of the opposite sex," Bacani said, noting that the club offers museum tours and other cultural events as well. "We're trying to become the Arch Deluxe of church groups, to appeal to a more mature, refined taste."

27 Rev. Terry Keehan, 40, associate pastor of Queen of Angels Catholic Church in Chicago, helped start the Ravenswood 20s and 30s a little more than a year ago. The group, for singles and married couples, mainly involves people from Queen of Angels and St. Benedict's, but also draws from nine different parishes in and around the Ravenswood area.

28 Keehan said he has noticed a big shift in what young adults want from their church. "They still like to party. They still like the social events," he said. "But it's more overt that they say, 'I really want something spiritual.'"

29 Hence, the Ravenswood group follows every mass with a social event. One time it might be karaoke. Another might be bowling. After one mass the group went to *The Rocky Horror Picture Show*. The idea, Keehan said, is, "Let's gather together. Let's pray. And then let's have some fun."

Chicago Tribune

Postreading

I. Getting the Message

After reading the article, choose the best answer for each item.

1. The main idea of the article is that churches
   a. are trying to appeal to single people.
   b. are criticizing the way single people live.
   c. are encouraging single people to get married.

2. One reason that some singles groups go to bars and restaurants is to
   a. find out how other people live.
   b. reject traditional teachings.
   c. create a feeling of community.

3. In addition to having fun, the St. Michael's Social Club
   a. requires that all members attend church every weekend.
   b. does community service work.
   c. contributes money to political organizations.

4. One reason for the new interest in religious groups for young adults is
   a. the tendency of many to get married later in life.
   b. the tendency of many to get married earlier in life.
   c. young single people are more serious today than previously.

5. More than married people, many singles feel a need to
   a. have fun.
   b. meet people.
   c. have a spiritual life.

6. Some of those interviewed in this article emphasize that churches
   a. are financial as well as spiritual organizations.
   b. are communities.
   c. are changing their church services and rituals.

7. The purpose of the article is to
   a. tell readers where the best church singles groups are.
   b. explain what church singles groups are currently doing.
   c. encourage readers to join church singles groups.

Check your answers with the key on page 165. If you have made mistakes, reread the article to gain a better understanding of it.

II. Expanding Your Vocabulary

A. Getting Meaning from Context

Use context clues to determine the meaning of each word or phrase in the paragraphs indicated in parentheses. Choose the correct definition.

1. filing (1)   a. arranging files   b. walking in a line
2. enduring (3)   a. bearing pain   b. finishing
3. disaffected (4)   a. made discontented   b. made affectionate
4. tenets (5)   a. songs   b. beliefs
5. eschewing (7)   a. doing   b. avoiding
6. buttress (7)   a. understand   b. support
7. figure (8)   a. think   b. shape, form
8. intimidating (22) a. frightening   b. fun

Chicago Tribune

Postreading

B. Matching Opposites
Match each word with its opposite. Use a dictionary if necessary.

1. _____ solemnity
2. _____ hedonistic
3. _____ gloomy
4. _____ ultimately
5. _____ acknowledging
6. _____ contemporary
7. _____ sacred
8. _____ refined
9. _____ overt

a. initially
b. covert
c. ancient
d. ignoring
e. secular
f. happy
g. self-denying
h. hilarity
i. crude

III. Working with Idioms and Expressions

Study the meanings of the idioms and expressions below. A form of each one appears in the paragraph indicated in parentheses.

make a pitch (2) try to sell or persuade
in keeping with (5) in agreement with something
drive off (7) force away
finger-wagging (7) irritating criticism
fire-and-brimstone (7) a style of speech in which the preacher talks about the terrible consequences of immoral behavior
abide by (9) obey
kosher cooking (11) cooking according to Jewish laws
head off (12) go
pitch in (12) help energetically
take up time (18) use up or fill up time
get away from (26) reject; disassociate oneself from
draw from (27) get or obtain from

Complete the sentences below with idioms and expressions from the list above.

1. Church groups that do service work helping people in the city like members who _____ when a job has to be done.

2. A person who belongs to a conservative church sometimes finds it hard to _____ the church's strict moral teachings.

3. Clergy who are trying to win new church members do not want to _____ people by criticizing them or making religion seem grim.

4. Some church singles groups want to _____ the popular idea that their purpose is just to help members find dates.

Postreading

IV. Analyzing Paragraphs

In a well-written article such as this one, each paragraph or set of paragraphs accomplishes a specific purpose. Reread the paragraphs indicated below in parentheses and try to understand their function and the type of information they provide. Then answer the questions.

1. Paragraphs 1 through 3 introduce the subject of the article. These paragraphs describe a scene rather than explain the purpose of the article. Is this a good way to begin? Why or why not?
2. Paragraph 4, which describes how churches need to nurture young adults, acts as a kind of topic sentence for paragraphs 5, 6, 7, and 8. Name one thing churches are doing—and one thing churches are avoiding—in order to nurture single people.
3. Which of the following is the main topic for paragraphs 9 through 15—the practice of going to bars, the usefulness of cooking classes, the need for community, or the problems of Jewish singles groups?
4. Paragraphs 16 through 18 give several reasons why more singles groups have been formed recently. What reason does Rabbi Charles Savenor give?
5. Paragraphs 19 and 20 explain how the Graduate and Professional division of The Hillels of Illinois uses a rather different approach from that of the other organizations mentioned in the article. What is their approach?
6. Paragraphs 21 through 24 relate the example of a single woman's solution to the problem of making friends in a church. How did she solve her problem?
7. Paragraphs 25 through 28 give two examples of groups that are trying to "change the perception that they are merely places to get dates." What are these groups doing?
8. Paragraph 29 concludes the article with a new example of a group's activities. Is this a good conclusion? Can you think of another way to conclude the article?

V. Talking and Writing

Discuss the questions below. Then choose one of them to write about.

1. Do churches act as centers of community life in your native country? Compare and contrast the importance of religion in your native country with its importance in the United States.
2. What are the special problems that single people face living in a big city? How can a church help with those problems?
3. Do churches have "singles groups" in your native country? Do they make special attempts to encourage single people to join the church or to keep them in? How do people from your native country feel about men and women meeting through a church or religious organization?

Chicago Tribune

Preparation

Religious groups push campaign fund reforms

Previewing the Article

Government and religion have an uneasy relationship in the United States. People believe in the separation of church and state, but in real life they find it difficult to keep the two separate.

Campaign financing, as this article shows, is one area where people in the United States face this dilemma. In order to get elected, politicians need a lot of money. A political campaign for a national office such as the Senate or Congress requires expensive radio and television advertising. Political parties pay for this with support from wealthy *interest groups* such as business and organized labor and *lobbying groups* such as the NRA (the National Rifle Association) and the AARP (the American Association of Retired Persons). As a result of their campaign support, large, powerful groups such as these usually have enormous influence on legislation.

But great influence from rich interest groups means less influence from churches. One result of this situation, for example, is that politicians are usually much more concerned with the U.S. tobacco industry than with a church's protest of China's treatment of Buddhists in Tibet. There are campaign finance laws that seek to limit the influence of rich contributors, but they have had very little effect.

This article is about an organized attempt by religious groups to change campaign finance laws so that politicians can direct their attention to moral and social issues of concern to churches. The union of these diverse churches for a single political purpose is an example of the old expression "Politics makes strange bedfellows." This means that people who normally disagree often find, through political battles of one type or another, that they have a common interest.

Before You Read

Before you read, discuss the following questions:

1. How are elections financed in your native country? Are politicians afraid of offending rich contributors?
2. How much influence do churches have on politics in your native country?
3. If, as a resident of the United States, you wanted a U.S. senator to support a concern of yours, how would you try to influence the senator? Do you think you could have any effect on U.S. legislation?

As You Read

As you read, try to explain why the group described in the article is called the "Dollars and Democracy Project."

Religious groups push campaign fund reforms

By Steve Kloehn
TRIBUNE RELIGION WRITER

1   Add the following special interest groups to the list of organizations fighting for campaign finance reform: Quakers, Catholics, Jews, evangelical Christians, Muslims and mainline Protestants.

2   Representatives of all those faiths, from a handful of Midwestern cities, have joined together to demand an overhaul of laws governing political contributions.

3   Organizers of the Dollars and Democracy Project announced Wednesday that they plan to hold 300 citizen meetings in Illinois and Ohio over the next year in an effort to create grass-roots momentum for reform at the national and state levels.

4   If campaign financing sounds like an arcane corner of public life to target for a religious crusade, leaders of the Dollars and Democracy Project said that it undercuts a host of more traditional religious concerns, from soup kitchens to health care.

5   "If this is unaddressed, all the social justice and peace issues that we care so much about will become less and less a priority for those in (public) office," Tom Choquette of the Roman Catholic Archdiocese of Cincinnati told more than 80 people who gathered at the Chicago Temple First United Methodist Church for the announcement.

6   The organizers posted 10 "moral and religious principles" they believe campaign finance reform should follow, focusing primarily on making politics equally accessible and accountable to all people.

7   "It's easy to understand and say you shouldn't favor the wealthy—anybody can say it—yet that's what we do in this country," said Rabbi Robert Marx, founder of the Jewish Council on Urban Affairs in Chicago.

8   Like Marx, many of the speakers cited Bible passages they believe support the Dollars and Democracy principles.

9   At least one supporter acknowledged that the principles—such as putting the common good ahead of corporate interests and giving candidates equal access to voters—are nothing new in the campaign finance debate. But Jim Wallis, founder of Call to Renewal, a national network of socially active Christians, said that innovation is not the point.

10   "Washington is full of good ideas and bad public policy," Wallis said. "What we need is momentum."

11   The project is funded by the non-profit Joyce Foundation of Chicago.

Postreading

I. Getting the Message

After reading the article, indicate if each statement below is true (T) or false (F).

1. _____ The purpose of this article is to argue the author's opinion about the influence of religious groups.
2. _____ The Dollars and Democracy Project is financed by large American corporations.
3. _____ Thousands of people listened to the announcement from the "Dollars and Democracy Project."
4. _____ The church representatives referred to in the article believe that big business has too much influence on politics in the United States.
5. _____ The main emphasis of the group's ten principles is that churches should receive just as much financial support from the government as corporations do.
6. _____ The Dollars and Democracy Project includes representatives from many different churches.
7. _____ The representatives at this meeting came from cities all over the United States and Canada.

Check your answers with the key on page 165. If you have made mistakes, reread the article to gain a better understanding of it.

II. Expanding Your Vocabulary

Getting Meaning from Context

Find each word in the paragraph indicated in parentheses. Use context clues to determine the meaning of the word. Choose the best definition.

1. mainline (1)
   a. minor, marginal
   b. major, widely accepted
2. overhaul (2)
   a. avoidance
   b. major revision
3. arcane (4)
   a. old
   b. obscure
4. target (4)
   a. perform in a contest
   b. mark as a goal
5. undercuts (4)
   a. undermines
   b. sells cheaply
6. host (4)
   a. a large number
   b. a person who has a party
7. cited (8)
   a. quoted
   b. saw
8. momentum (10)
   a. new ideas
   b. growing strength
9. funded (11)
   a. supported financially
   b. discovered

Chicago Tribune

Postreading

III. Working with Idioms and Expressions

Study the meaning of the idioms and expressions below. A form of each one appears in the paragraphs indicated in parentheses.

special interest group (1) a group of people that seeks special legislation favorable to the group

campaign finance reform (1) reform of campaign finance law that would effectively limit the power of rich contributors by limiting how much they can contribute

a handful of (2) a small number of

grass-roots (3) involving the common people, not the rich and powerful

sound like (4) appear to be the same as

soup kitchens (4) places that supply free meals to homeless and poor people

the common good (9) the benefit of everyone, not just of a special group

equal access (9) the ability of politicians to contact and speak with all people equally, not just the rich

nothing new (9) a familiar and unsurprising thing

Answer the following questions:

1. In paragraph 1 how would *campaign finance reform* help the religious groups?
2. In paragraph 3 how do the religious groups propose getting *grass-roots* support for their cause?
3. In paragraph 9 do you think it is hard or easy to determine *the common good*? Why?
4. In paragraph 9 why are the principles of Dollars and Democracy called *nothing new*?

IV. Making Sense of Sentences

Finding Subjects and Verbs

To understand long sentences that contain many phrases and modifiers, it is useful to locate the subjects and verbs. These are the core of the sentence. Some sentences have only one subject-verb pair, but others have several. Each subject-verb pair is called a *clause*.

For example, paragraph 3 contains two subject-verb pairs and thus two clauses: 1. "Organizers . . . announced"; 2. "they plan"

To find the verb, figure out which words indicate an action (*John* runs *fast* or *Linda* studies *hard*) or a state of being (*Ellen* is *nice* or *Mr. Smith* seems *confused*).

To find the subject, figure out which word indicates the doer of the action (as in *John* runs fast or *Mary* studies hard) or the person or thing associated with the state of being expressed by the verb (as in *Ellen* is nice or *Mr. Smith* seems confused).

Chicago Tribune

Postreading

In this exercise find the verbs and the subjects in each sentence. The first one has been done for you.

1. (Paragraph 2, main clause) Verb: _____ *have joined* _____   Subject: _____ *Representatives* _____

2. (Paragraph 4, 1st clause) Verb: _____   Subject: _____

   (2nd clause)   Verb: _____   Subject: _____

3. (Paragraph 6, 1st clause) Verb: _____   Subject: _____

   (2nd clause)   Verb: _____   Subject: _____

4. (Paragraph 8, 1st clause) Verb: _____   Subject: _____

   (2nd clause)   Verb: _____   Subject: _____

V. Talking and Writing

Discuss the topics below. Then choose one of them to write about.

1. Do you think religious groups should become involved in politics the way the Dollars and Democracy Project has? Why or why not?

2. Why do you think elected officials are slow to reform campaign financing? Can you think of any examples from the news that illustrate this problem?

3. Do you think the rich special interest groups prevent the common people from having a voice in the political system? Why or why not?

Chicago Tribune

Focus on Culture

Setting the Scene

Newspapers reflect the religious culture of their readers. In Chicago, for example, the largest single organized religion is Roman Catholicism. This is because of the large number of Chicagoans of Polish, Irish, and Latino background. Thus many more stories appear in the *Chicago Tribune* about Catholic matters than would appear in a newspaper located in some other area of the country such as the South or the West, regions that have fewer Catholics. In this way, newspapers provide great clues to the religious culture of their readers—their spiritual values, moral attitudes, habits of worship, and even the social, educational, and political importance of religious matters.

Types of Religion Articles

You will find that a large daily newspaper contains many different kinds of articles about religious matters, including the following:

- **Local news stories** about important church meetings, church-related demonstrations or protests, scandals, deaths of church leaders, and the choice of new church leaders
- **International news stories** about religious and ethnic wars, papal visits, interfaith meetings, and international conventions
- **Profiles** of important church leaders, writers on religious topics, and active church members
- **Business and financial stories** about churches and their real estate holdings and financial status
- **Education stories** about church-supported elementary schools, high schools, and colleges
- **Feature stories** about local churches, church history, problems that churches face in gaining new members or new clergy, theological issues, and many other matters
- **Holiday stories** that appear regularly throughout the year about what particular church members do on important religious feasts such as Christmas, Ramadan, or Passover
- **Book reviews** of works on religious topics
- **Arts and Entertainment stories** about stage performances, films, music, and art associated with churches
- **Cult stories** that deal with the sometimes vague line between organized religions and other kinds of unofficial or unrecognized religious groups, commonly referred to as *cults*

Chicago Tribune

Focus on Culture

Exercise 1. Journal Assignment: Culture Comparison

For two weeks scan your local newspaper for the kinds of stories listed on page 124.
Fill out the chart below by answering the following questions: 1. What is the headline?
2. What kind of article is it? 3. Was the article interesting to you? (Yes or No) 4. Would
this kind of article appear in a newspaper in your native country? (Yes or No)

	Headline	Kind	Interesting?	In Your Native Country?
1.				
2.				
3.				
4.				
5.				
6.				

Exercise 2. Analyzing a Religion Article

Choose the most interesting article from those listed above and answer the following
questions:
1. How does the headline help you predict the content and viewpoint of the article?
2. What is the purpose of the article (to explain, to argue, to report, etc.)?
3. What is the main idea of the article?
4. Is the article difficult to understand? Why?
5. What makes the article interesting or uninteresting to you?
6. Does the article tell you anything new about the religious values of the people in
   the local community? What does it tell you?

Chicago Tribune

Focus on Culture

Exercise 3. The Language of Religion

Each individual religious faith has its own vocabulary, which may not be known to people outside the faith. For example, Christians may not be familiar with Muslim terms such as *Ramadan, Haj,* or *Mevlud;* Protestants may not know Roman Catholic terms such as *high mass, monsignor,* or *holy orders.* In reporting about religion, newspapers use specific vocabulary that may not be understood by all readers.

For this exercise you need to read two or three articles that deal significantly with a religious issue. Write down at least three sentences that include religious terms you don't know, and underline the terms. Discuss the terms in class and see if you can define them. Research the meanings of any terms you can't define.

Exercise 4. The Newspaper, Religion, and You

Few issues discussed in newspapers affect readers as directly and personally as articles about religion do. When we read news about distant wars, earthquakes, and movie stars, our emotions are not usually affected. But when we read a story that touches upon our religious beliefs, we can react more strongly.

Find an article that deals with your own religion (or with a religion that you are very familiar with). Answer the following questions about the article:
1. What is the main idea of the article?
2. Are the facts and details in the article true as far as you can tell?
3. Who is the intended audience of the article? Does the author explain terms that you already know? Does the author assume the reader already knows specific religious vocabulary?
4. Is the writer objective, or do you detect some kind of bias?

Chicago Tribune

1

Enough of these holidays!
Your body is set to give up

2

School's still out, but
for parents, it's no vacation

3

Sick of your house?
Do we have a home for you!

Focus on Culture

At Home

Chicago Tribune

At Home

The Evolving Notion of Home

"Home, sweet home" is a phrase that expresses an essential attitude in the United States. Whether the reality of life in the family house is sweet or not so sweet, the cherished ideal of home has great importance for many people.

This ideal is a vital part of the American dream. This dream, dramatized in the history of nineteenth-century European settlers of the American West, was to find a piece of land, build a house for one's family, and start a farm. These small households were portraits of independence: the entire family—mother, father, children, even grandparents—living in a small house and working together to support each other. Everyone understood the life and death importance of family cooperation and hard work.

Although most people in the United States no longer live on farms, the ideal of home ownership is just as strong in the twentieth century as it was in the nineteenth. When U.S. soldiers came home after World War II, for example, they dreamed of buying houses and starting families. So there was a tremendous boom in home building. The new houses, typically in the suburbs, were often small and nearly identical, but they satisfied a deep need. Many saw the single-family house as the basis of their way of life.

For the new suburbanites of the 1950s and 1960s, however, life inside their small houses was very different from life on a farm. First, the family spent much less time together in the house. The father frequently drove, or *commuted,* as much as an hour to work each morning. The children went to school all day and played after school with neighborhood children. The suburb itself was sometimes called a *bedroom community* because people used their houses basically for sleeping. Second, the suburb frequently was not a stable community: families moved frequently as the fathers sought *upward mobility*—better-paying jobs and bigger houses. Although the idea of home was still as precious as always, it had taken on a different meaning.

In the seventies and eighties, as more women entered the labor force, the family spent even less time together. But the picture is changing: people can now *telecommute,* or work at home, while being linked to the office by means of their computer. More and more people can now stay at home. So the old expression could change from "Home, sweet home" to "Home, sweet office," but the emphasis on the cherished home will most likely stay the same.

Chicago Tribune

Preparation

Enough of these holidays! Your body is set to give up

Previewing the Article

"There's No Place Like Home for the Holidays." This is the title of a popular song of the Christmas and New Year's holiday season. It suggests the importance of the idea of home in the United States. For many people home is more than just a place; it is the center of an ideal of family happiness.

But the reality of the home at holiday time can be very different from the dream. Part of the problem is the importance of the Christmas and New Year's season itself. People in the United States expect a lot from the holidays. They spend money, go to parties, and get together with family members. They eat, drink, and play—and even watch TV and sleep—with greater enthusiasm and higher hopes than at any other time of the year. And all this happy activity is centered in the home.

But as this interesting article relates, many people, because of their busy schedules, are not used to spending so much time relaxing and playing at home away from their normal work and school routines. People in the United States like to *think* of their culture as centered in the home, but for many their jobs are the center of their lives. This contrast has some surprising results: first, holiday fun at home can become oddly tiresome; second, people can actually begin looking forward to going back to work; third, the shift back to a work schedule can be emotionally and physically difficult to handle.

Before You Read

Discuss the following questions:
1. Read the headline. Why would a person's body be "set to give up" because of holiday activity?
2. Are holiday vacations ever a disappointment to you? Why?
3. Think of your experience and observation of U.S. life during the Christmas and New Year's season. How important is this time of year to people in the United States? For example, how extensive are the decorations on homes and businesses? How important is the season to retail stores?

As You Read

Look for the term *internal body clock* and think about how this term can explain the discomfort we feel in the transition from vacation to work.

Enough of these holidays!
Your body is set to give up

The Chicago Children's Museum might be a great place to visit over the New Year's holiday, but whiling away the hours while off from work or school can be disruptive to the mind and body.
Photo by Steve Kagan.

By Cindy Schreuder
TRIBUNE STAFF WRITER

1 You're off work, and hanging out at home.

2 Off your diet and into cookies, big dinners and champagne.

3 Off your schedule, and up nights with Letterman, Leno or a good book.

4 Off your workout routine and skipping your morning swim or evening run.

5 In short, you're off, blissfully free of responsibilities and pressure, stuffed full of food and fun. And you don't like it.

6 "All humans, and for that matter all species that are vertebrates and many that are not, have an internal clock mechanism," said George Brainard, professor of neurology at Thomas Jefferson University in Philadelphia. "That's not a metaphor. It's an actual biological entity."

7 As many people find themselves in the second week of enforced indolence because of the winter break—whether because of school holidays or time off from work—more than a few may be experiencing a peculiar sensation:

8 A twinge or even a wave of discontent at the luxury of doing

nothing, of sitting around with time to spare, the commodity of the late 20th Century that we're constantly told is in dangerously short supply.

9   The sense is that you should feel great, but actually you don't. You hate to admit it, but it might even be a welcome break to go back to work or school.

10   "I enjoy being off, but I enjoy coming back too," said Virginia Woodard of Chicago.

11   After several days off around Christmas, she was back at her baby-sitting job on New Year's Eve, taking her 3-year-old charge to a museum.

12   "It messes up your schedule, and coming back is tiresome," said Woodard, who nonetheless said she enjoyed her time off.

13   "I feel like I'll need a week to recover to get back on my schedule," said Joni Lederer. She and her family shared the holidays at their Highland Park home with an out-of-state family, and she has spent the days since taking her two sons skating, bowling and to museums.

14   There is a body of research behind the discombobulation, a scientific way of saying blame biology for the blahs.

15   "Most people," said Brainard, "do better and are healthier if they keep a regular social calendar to their life that is somewhat consistent with their internal timekeeping mechanism."

16   The changes in routine that commonly occur during the holidays come at a biological cost. Those changes disrupt the body clock, located primarily in the brain, and may produce an out-of-sorts feeling akin to singing a half-step off-key.

17   "Normal day-to-day routines and realities are very supportive of the internal clock structure that leads to optimal health," he added.

18   "We've come over from England, so we've interrupted our routine completely," said Barry Neale, who spent part of Tuesday sightseeing and shopping for books.

19   Added his wife, Donna Neale, "Everything from when you get up to when you can get in the bathroom changes."

20   But she cautioned that she wasn't complaining, adding, "Change can be as good as rest."

21   Further complicating matters, these schedule disruptions happen around the winter solstice, when days are short and, in places such as Chicago, often cloudy. Light is the best reset mechanism for the human biological clock. But cold, gray and sloppy winter weather tends to keep people indoors, where light levels are especially low.

22   "Light indoors, in most homes and offices, is equivalent to biological darkness. You can see everything, but your body does not register it as daylight," Brainard said.

23   The tendency to drift from a regular schedule during the holidays is aided and abetted by modern mores: Most people don't get enough sleep during the workweek and try to make up for it during days off, further disrupting their body clock's calibration.

24   "We are a sleep-deprived population," said Margarita Dubocovich, a neuropharmacologist at Northwestern University. "Studies say people sleep one hour less (a night) now than they used to sleep 10 or 15 years ago. You accumulate this sleep deprivation."

25   Being off-schedule—or, as scientists say, "out of phase"—can produce feelings of listlessness, irritability and, in severe cases, depression.

26   "Whatever you do that upsets your rhythms affects your moods," said Mark Rea, director of the Lighting Research Center at Rensselaer Polytechnic Institute in Troy, N.Y. "If you have long nights and darker days, you're not getting your full dose of light to make your (body) clock start at the right time."

27   In this, the season of material gifts, consider the extra time a gift. Spend it on things for which you don't normally have time, psychologists suggest.

28   One possibility is to accomplish something tangible, such as eliminating the clutter in your home or workplace.

29   "When our surroundings are cluttered, we tend to feel overwhelmed," said Ronald Nathan, a psychologist who is a professor of family practice at the Albany Medical College in Albany, N.Y. "By clearing the view, you can feel more capable and confident."

30   Other people feel best if they follow more contemplative or spiritual pursuits, such as meditating or praying, Nathan said.

31   Even such things as the ubiquitous holiday football bowl games can provide a mental lift and a feeling of structure.

32   "Ballgames are a way to narrow the stimuli and focus and have a structure that the day fails to offer," said Nathan, who is a co-author of books on managing stress, including, *The Doctor's Guide to Instant Stress Relief.*

33   Time off during the holidays, however endless it may seem, will end. The day of reckoning, when school reopens or work resumes, looms near the top of that brand new calendar.

34   To ease the transition, researchers who study human biological rhythms say, it is best to gradually reset the body's clock. Do this by going to sleep a little earlier at night, waking a little earlier in the morning and getting back on a typical schedule.

35   Although that is the best way, researchers know from scientific and personal experience that it is probably not the most common way.

36   More typically, people wait until the last minute, reverting to their old routine the night before returning to work or to school.

37   So procrastinate if you must. Just don't moan about how out-of-sorts you feel on Monday to friends and family who have spent the last two weeks at work.

Chicago Tribune
Postreading

I. Getting the Message

After reading the article, choose the best answer for each item.

1. The main idea of this article is that
   a. time off of work can upset people physically and emotionally.
   b. vacations are a bad idea and should be avoided.
   c. people should get more sleep during the holidays.

2. The purpose of the article is
   a. to describe the attitude people in the United States have toward work.
   b. to explain why people can feel upset during the holidays and suggest remedies.
   c. to argue against the practice of taking time off work during the New Year's holidays.

3. Researchers say that during a vacation people should
   a. work very hard.
   b. avoid all tiring activities as much as possible.
   c. create a schedule of leisure activities.

4. According to researchers, sunlight is important because it
   a. keeps our biological clocks set on a healthy schedule.
   b. is necessary to avoid diseases of the eye.
   c. helps us to see things more clearly than artificial light.

5. Lack of enough sleep, or "sleep deprivation," can
   a. be a good thing because it allows people to get more work done.
   b. be cured by sleeping extra hours every weekend.
   c. produce irritability and depression.

6. According to one researcher, watching football games on TV during the holidays
   a. can be too stimulating and have a negative effect on relaxation.
   b. is bad because it is too great a departure from regular work schedules.
   c. can give a little bit of healthy structure to vacation days.

7. Going back to work after a vacation break is difficult mainly because
   a. nobody really likes to work.
   b. vacations are always wonderful and relaxing.
   c. it is hard to get the body back into a work schedule.

Check your answers with the key on page 165. If you have made mistakes, reread the article to gain a better understanding of it.

II. Expanding Your Vocabulary

A. Getting Meaning from Context

Find each word in the paragraph indicated in parentheses. Use context clues to determine the meaning of the word. Choose the best definition.

1. indolence (7)   a. work   b. laziness
2. discontent (8)   a. uselessness   b. unhappiness
3. commodity (8)   a. useful thing   b. time
4. discombobulation (14) a. upset   b. activity
5. optimal (17)   a. not necessary   b. best
6. mores (23)   a. ways of living   b. additional things
7. tangible (28)   a. spiritual   b. practical

Postreading

8. ubiquitous (31)	a. dangerous	b. appearing everywhere
9. reverting (36)	a. going back	b. seeing again
10. procrastinate (37)	a. delay until later	b. work hard

B. Recognizing Suffixes

Suffixes are groups of letters placed at the ends of words. Often suffixes change the part of speech of the original word. For example, the suffixes *-ness, -ity,* and *-sion,* used in paragraph 25, are noun endings. The suffix *-ness* changes the adjective *listless* into a noun, *listlessness;* the suffix *-ity* changes the adjective *irritable* into a noun, *irritability;* the suffix *-sion* changes the verb *depress* into a noun, *depression.*

For this exercise find the word ending in *-ness, -ity*, or *-sion (-tion)* in the paragraph indicated in the column on the left. Write the suffix, the noun formed by the suffix, and the original word that the suffix changes. The first one has been done for you.

		Suffix	Noun	Original Word
1.	Paragraph 5	-ity	responsibilities	responsible
2.	Paragraph 7			
3.	Paragraph 8			
4.	Paragraph 14			
5.	Paragraph 21			

III. Working with Idioms and Expressions

Study the meanings of the idioms and expressions below. A form of each one appears in the indicated paragraph of the article.

hang out (1) spend time

Letterman and **Leno** (3) Jay Leno and David Letterman are popular comedian-hosts of late-night television shows

in short supply (8) very small amount remaining

mess up (12) cause confusion

get back on schedule (13) return to normal routine

out-of-sorts (16) irritable, in low spirits

akin to (16) similar to, related to

winter solstice (21) December 21st, the beginning of winter in the Northern Hemisphere

season of material gifts (27) the gift-giving season of Christmas and New Year's

day of reckoning (33) a day in the future when obligations must be met

Postreading

Complete the sentences below with the idioms and expressions above.

1. A holiday routine of going to parties and staying out late can really _____ a person's ability to cope with a normal work schedule later.

2. About the time of the _____ some people become tired and depressed partly because of lack of sunlight.

3. The first day of work is a _____ for people who have changed their normal schedule completely over the holidays.

4. Psychologists recommend that the best way to _____ after the holidays is to gradually start returning to your normal routine several days before the first day of work.

IV. Focusing on Style and Tone

The introduction of a newspaper article is called the *lead.* The lead in a news story gives the important facts by answering the questions *who, what, when, where,* and *why.* The main purpose is to keep the reader interested.

Reread paragraphs 1–5, the *lead* of this article, and answer the following questions.

1. Is this an effective way to begin the article? Why?
2. The writer uses the second person—*you*—instead of the more common third person—*he, she, it,* or *they*—which is mainly used in the rest of the article. Is the second person effective? What advantages does it have?
3. The writer uses specific examples like cookies, champagne, and late-night TV. Are these good examples? Can you think of others?
4. The lead ends with the sentence "And you don't like it." Is this statement a surprise? Why?
5. Which of the following words would you use to describe the tone of the lead—*formal, instructional* (or *didactic*), *conversational,* or *argumentative*? Explain.

V. Talking and Writing

Discuss the topics below. Then choose one of them to write about.

1. How important is the Christmas and New Year's season in your native country? In what ways is the season viewed differently?
2. How does an at-home New Year's Eve party in the United States differ from one in your native country? Discuss similarities and differences with regard to food, decorations, drink, music, dancing, conversation, games, and the invitation list.
3. Is the situation described in the article—the fact that people can grow tired of holiday "fun"—a common one in your native country? Are people eager to get back to work after the holidays?

Preparation

Chicago Tribune

School's still out, but for parents, it's no vacation

Previewing the Article

Thirty or forty years ago, when most mothers in the United States didn't have jobs, homes were busier places. Children went to school from 9 A.M. to 3 P.M. and spent the rest of the time in the house under their mother's watchful eyes. Children played, watched TV, and did homework, and when they weren't in the house, they were outside in the front or back yard or playing nearby with other neighborhood children.

Though this situation still exists in some communities today, it is becoming rarer and rarer as more and more mothers have work outside the home. These "two-income families" create a different kind of home—one that is a place to stop by temporarily in the midst of a busy schedule of activities. Because working parents often leave the house by 8 A.M. and return at 5 or 6 P.M., children go to school and then to a series of highly-programmed after-school activities. So when school lets out for two or three weeks at New Year's time, many parents may face a troubling situation.

This article shows the kind of child-care problem the holidays can create for busy parents. Even in those families in which the mother is home, there is often no active neighborhood full of children playing since most of the other children are involved in activities. This results in the irony of both parents and children anxiously looking forward to the end of their vacation.

Before You Read

Discuss the following questions:
1. Does the New Year's holiday break pose special problems for your family? If so, describe them.
2. Have you ever baby-sat with pre-school-age children for a few days? Was it difficult to do? Why?
3. In your native country, are there widespread organized activities for children during school breaks? Why or why not?

As You Read

As you read, count the number of named suburban cities or towns. Why did the authors refer to all of these instead of just one?

School's still out,
but for parents, it's no vacation

With schools and colleges out, there's time for hockey in Schaumburg with (from top to bottom) Brandon Young, 12; Ed Heidler, 21; Pete Lapin, 17; and Stew Wing, 22. Stephen Shannon, 12, looks on. Tribune photo by Chuck Berman.

By Lou Carlozo and Pam Cytrynbaum
TRIBUNE STAFF WRITERS

TRIBUNE REPORTER LYNN VAN MATRE
CONTRIBUTED TO THIS ARTICLE.

1   For Monica Palm of Libertyville, the most challenging phase of the holiday season begins long after the presents beneath the tree have been opened.

2   Through the end of the week, Palm's 8-year-old twin boys, Marty and Mike, are off from school. For Palm, 39, a single working mother, that means juggling her work schedule to get time off, then a week of brainstorming, improvising and arranging fun activities for the kids.

3   As she listed Wednesday's game plan—which would either include a visit to Navy Pier's "Earthquake Room" or a luncheon party for the boys and some neighborhood friends—Palm paused to wonder where her own vacation went.

4   "It's like I have no life," she said.

5   Palm's plight illustrates a situation many Chicago-area parents face this week, as quirky schedules have students in some suburban school districts off as late as Jan. 8—even though Christmas, Hanukkah and New Year's Day are history.

6   For parents staying at home, the problem centers on what can be done to keep kids entertained. For working parents, the chal-

lenge may simply be what to do with the kids.

7   In some areas, malls become the magnets where teens are left to roam free and spend their leftover Christmas money (or in some rare instances, indulge a parent's credit card).

8   It's also a time of year when grandparents find themselves pressed into service, as their children return to work, and their children's children drop by for extended visits.

9   There are many families, of course, where relatives or willing neighbors simply aren't there to watch the children. So in communities such as Downers Grove, Evanston, Palatine and Villa Park,

local officials have responded to the post-holiday predicament with recreation programs specifically tailored for this time of year.

10   The activities are part-entertainment, part–baby-sitting, with the unofficial mission of staving off that timeless adolescent war cry, "I'm bored."

11   "We try to offer programs that fill the gap, to help parents go to work and not worry about the kids watching themselves," said Martha Logan, a spokeswoman for Evanston's Division of Recreation.

12   Evanston's "Winter Sports Camp," open to ages 6 to 12, operates during the two weeks Evanston School District 65 is on Christmas break.

13   For $118 a week, Evanston parents can leave their children at the Chandler-Newberger Sports Center at 9:30 A.M. and not worry about picking them up until 4 P.M.

14   If those hours are inconvenient, the city offers additional baby-sitting services, running as early as 7:15 A.M. and late as 6 P.M., at the frugal rate of $1 per hour.

15   Activities run the gamut from basketball and floor hockey to bowling and roller skating. There is even a planned trip to a video arcade, Logan said.

16   In DuPage County, the Downers Grove Park District holds a similar winter camp that opened Dec. 26 and will continue through Friday. And in Villa Park, children 8 to 12 can enroll in the Park District's Winter Adventure Camp, which opened Dec. 27 and continues through Friday.

17   Not all the post-holiday sports are necessarily organized. For Pete Lapin, a 17-year-old student at Schaumburg High School, the extra time off meant a chance to meet some college-age friends at Volkening Lake for a pickup game of ice hockey.

18   In homes where at least one parent can stay home, this is either a week full of quality time, crafts, games, movies, museums, bumper bowling and birthday parties—or the week from hell.

19   For Laura Puente of Forest Park, the key word this week is "stretch" as she tries to entertain her 6-year-old, Alex.

20   "We're trying out all the Christmas toys Alex got, one . . . at . . . a . . . time," Puente said.

21   At the very least, it poses a creativity test for moms like Diane Star of Wheeling, who somehow manage to craft their own slate of exhaustive (and exhausting) diversions.

22   "I feel like I'm running my own day camp," Star said, "at home."

23   Tops on Star's list is a birthday party for her younger daughter, who turns 6 Thursday. Star scheduled the party during the week to give other adults a break from endless weekend birthdays and because her daughter's school friends are off too.

24   "I figured most parents would have nothing for the kids to do, so we thought, 'Let's have the party,'" said Star, who lives in Wheeling and is a physical education teacher.

25   As much as she enjoys the family time, Star acknowledged that she was anxious for school to resume.

26   "I'll tell you, Jan. 8 will be a relief," she said. "I'm going to need a vacation from my vacation."

27   Even some children admit to looking forward to the end of vacation.

28   Take 9-year-old Sarah Keister of Lake Zurich, who with sisters Mary and Margaret tagged along with grandmother Cleo Kohn at Hawthorn Center in Vernon Hills.

29   For Kohn at least, the plan of action sounded exciting: "We're going to have popcorn and movie parties, have crafts projects and play a lot of games," Kohn said.

30   But for Sarah, the thought of returning to her friends, favorite teachers, even her math books, seemed more inviting.

31   Perhaps a bit shy to discuss the issue in front of Grandma, Sarah smiled and said simply, "I'm ready to go back."

Meanwhile, Michael, 7, (left) and Ryan McCain, 5, participate in a Palatine Library program. Tribune photo by Nancy Stone.

Postreading

I. Getting the Message

After reading the article, choose the best answer for each item.

1. This article is mainly about
   a. the fun of the holiday season.
   b. how parents keep children busy during the holidays.
   c. park district recreation programs.

2. Park districts have daytime programs for children during the holidays because
   a. the children demand them.
   b. children are not in school and parents often aren't home.
   c. sports lessons are increasing in popularity.

3. Children can become bored during the holidays because
   a. they do not like park district activities.
   b. they are tired of seeing the same friends each day.
   c. it is hard to keep busy and have fun at home.

4. The main idea of the organized activities in the park districts is to
   a. keep children happy, busy, and safe.
   b. teach them skills they don't normally learn in school.
   c. make children more aware of the importance of sports.

5. During the holidays parents use malls as places
   a. to get some exercise.
   b. to encourage their children to look for bargains.
   c. to leave their children for the day.

Check your answers with the key on page 165. If you have made mistakes, reread the article to gain a better understanding of it.

II. Expanding Your Vocabulary

A. Getting Meaning from Context

Find each word below in the paragraph indicated in parentheses. Use context clues to determine the meaning of the word. Choose the best definition.

1. magnets (7)   a. electrical objects   b. attractive places
2. roam (7)   a. search   b. wander
3. frugal (14)   a. costing little   b. expensive
4. craft (21)   a. learn   b. make
5. slate (21)   a. list   b. organization
6. diversions (21)   a. classes   b. fun activities

B. Reading for Suggested Meanings

1. In paragraph 2 *brainstorming* and *improvising* are mentioned as necessary mental activities to create holiday activities for children. Look up these two words in a college dictionary. What is the difference in meaning? If you were having a picnic and it suddenly started to rain, would you *brainstorm* or *improvise*?

2. The words *plight* (paragraph 5) and *predicament* (paragraph 9) are synonyms. Look up both words in a college dictionary. Is there any difference in meaning? If a person were having trouble deciding whether to take a job or go to graduate school, would the situation be better described as a *plight* or a *predicament*?

Chicago Tribune

Postreading

3. Two adjectives formed from the verb *exhaust* are *exhaustive* and *exhausting* (paragraph 21). What is the difference between "*exhaustive* and *exhausting* diversions"?

III. Working with Idioms and Expressions

Study the meanings of the idioms and expressions below. A form of each one appears in the paragraph indicated in parentheses.

time off (2) vacation time or any period away from work

game plan (3) detailed strategy planned before an undertaking

history (5) in the past and no longer an issue

stave off (10) keep away

fill the gap (11) put something in a blank space; create meaningful activities

run the gamut (15) go the range of a subject

pickup game (17) a game in which the players are chosen informally just before the game

quality time (18) time parents spend attentively and actively with children

give someone a break (23) help someone have time to relax

look forward to (27) expect with pleasure

tag along (28) follow closely

Complete the sentences below with idioms and expressions from the list above.

1. Many parents need _____ from work at holiday time to watch their children who are home from school.

2. It is hard for a parent in charge of entertaining a small child to _____ the child's boredom for two weeks.

3. Busy working parents don't have much time to spend with their children, so they try to make sure that the moments that they do spend with them are _____ .

4. By the end of the holidays, parents often begin to _____ the beginning of school.

IV. Talking and Writing

Discuss the topics below. Then choose one of them to write about.

1. One reason for the problem described in the article is the decline of neighborhoods as places for children to play with each other. More and more children today are involved in organized activities after school, during holidays and summer vacations, and even on Saturdays. Is this a good thing or a bad thing? What are the advantages and disadvantages of organized activities?

2. If you were in charge of two children, ages four and six, for one week at the holidays, what would you do? Make up a schedule of activities.

Chicago Tribune

Preparation

Sick of your house? Do we have a home for you!

Previewing the Article

Is your house making you sick? This is the startling question posed in this article. As our understanding of pollution grows, we become more aware of how many different kinds of substances, some of them in our homes and offices, can hold and give off substances that cause allergies and other illnesses.

Aware of this fact, one enterprising builder has constructed a home that is designed to be free of any dangerous substances. The builder believes that as more and more Americans become aware of the various ways the environment can cause illness, more home buyers will be interested in such houses.

This goal of having a healthy house is a very typical one in the United States. Deep in U.S. culture is the restless belief that life can always be improved by taking action. Often, as in this case, the improvement comes through research and technological change. If your house is hurting you in subtle ways, then you must change the house. It is an at-home extension of the larger environmental movement, which claims that the survival of mankind depends on making our world a healthier place to live in.

The goal of having a healthy house also arises from the feeling—probably an international one—that a home should be a place of refuge, a safe little world different from the rougher world outside of it. The healthy-house movement strives to make a home safe in every sense of the word.

Before You Read

Before you read the article, answer the following questions:
1. Read the headline. What two meanings can you think of for the expression *sick of something*? What do people usually mean when they say they are sick of their house?
2. What do you know about allergies and what causes them? Have you heard of any allergy-causing substances in houses?
3. Have you ever felt that the physical environment of a building, such as an office or a store, made you feel sick? Describe the environment.

As You Read

At the end of this article the wife of the builder says, "People think you're nuts" to build this kind of house. As you read, ask yourself why some people might think this.

Sick of your house?
Do we have a home for you!

By Mary Umberger

1   If you visit the house that builder Tom Molidor is finishing up in Western Springs, please don't wear deodorant.

2   And don't even think of putting on perfume.

3   That's just the beginning of an unusual list of prohibitions, but then again, Molidor Custom Builders of Clarendon Hills is constructing an unusual house, and seeking an unusual buyer.

4   Outside, it's a conventional 2,600-square-foot brick structure. Inside, it's the "Healthy Home"—constructed free of materials that emit so-called "volatile organic compounds," resins or synthetic residues. It also has features designed to reduce sensitivity to allergies.

5   In other words, it's for somebody who wants a house that isn't likely to make its inhabitants sick. Visitors (and potential buyers) are asked to heed a posted list of substances that are forbidden in this veritable laboratory of the "healthy house" movement, which holds that most modern, tightly constructed houses are sources of torture to people with chemical sensitivities and certain allergies.

6   Molidor and his wife, Nancy, became unintentional participants in this movement several years ago after constructing their own home. Nancy developed a string of sinus infections, respiratory ailments and intestinal problems. As soon as one illness cleared up, another would appear, she says.

7   "My system was supersensitive," she explains, meaning that her house held in all manner of irritants that her body couldn't tolerate. Thus began a long process of modifying their home so that she could be comfortable in it.

8   The process was an education for both of them, and Tom decided that there might be a market for what they had learned. Last week, Molidor Custom Builders unveiled a division called the Healing Environment that will specialize in homes and room additions that are free of substances that some regard as toxic.

9   At the same time, he is finishing up the Western Springs house and looking for a buyer for the four-bedroom, $529,000 home.

10   The Healthy Home may be most notable for features that it lacks: carpeting, for instance. Molidor says the house has specially sealed hardwood floors because carpet may cause irritation two ways: Synthetic fibers may "offgas," or slowly release irritants; they also may trap substances that trigger allergies.

11   Painted, wooden cabinets are promised to be emission-free, lacking the plastic laminates, formaldehyde and glues that are common in contemporary cabinetmaking.

12   In the basement are devices to bring in fresh air and filter it, plus a whole-house vacuum system. The attached garage's roof has a ventilation fan to banish auto exhaust.

13   The house also has an elaborate water-filtration system. A humidistat monitors outdoor humidity to help adjust indoor humidity, in order to cope with mold growth.

14   Molidor researched building materials to find drywall, adhesives and taping compounds that wouldn't irritate. Ditto for the paints.

15   The research list goes on, down to the solvents that were used to peel away the forms that supported the concrete foundation as it was being poured.

16   Molidor said that such non-traditional materials and products, plus the time spent in locating and researching them, added $25,000 to $35,000 to the cost of the house, although he presumes that future projects won't have the same costly learning curve.

17   Although the couple have plenty of company in their conviction that houses can aggravate chemical sensitivities, some physicians remain unconvinced if not downright skeptical. Some say that more research needs to be done, others say that many such problems can be traced to more commonplace allergies or psychological problems.

18   "People think you're nuts," Nancy agrees, though she attributes those attitudes to medical naivete. She enumerates the ways she has changed her surroundings and daily life, from cleaning products to the fertilizers on her lawn, and offers a bottom line: "I don't feel sick now."

Chicago Tribune

Postreading

I. Getting the Message

After reading the article, indicate if each statement is true (T) or false (F).

1. _____ The builder of the nontoxic house has constructed many such homes.
2. _____ The builder does not want people to wear deodorant and perfume when they visit the house because these things contain chemicals that some people may be sensitive to.
3. _____ The builder's wife says that she learned through personal experience that substances in a house can cause illness.
4. _____ The house has hardwood floors because the builder believes carpeting is not attractive.
5. _____ Fresh air is brought into the house and filtered.
6. _____ Finding the right kind of building materials for the house made the house more expensive.
7. _____ Most medical doctors believe that people need to live in this kind of house to be free of allergies.
8. _____ The purpose of this article is to argue that this kind of house is the best kind to live in.

Check your answers with the key on page 165. If you have made mistakes, reread the article to gain a better understanding of it.

II. Expanding Your Vocabulary

A. Getting Meaning from Context

Find each word or phrase in the paragraph indicated in parentheses. Use context clues to determine the meaning of the word or phrase. Then choose the best definition.

1. prohibitions (3)   a. rules   b. advantages
2. torture (5)   a. confusion   b. great pain
3. string (6)   a. series   b. a very small number
4. supersensitive (7)   a. strong   b. very sensitive
5. notable (10)   a. hard to notice   b. remarkable
6. nontraditional (16)   a. normal   b. unusual
7. skeptical (17)   a. disbelieving   b. philosophical
8. naivete (18)   a. intelligence   b. simplicity, ignorance

B. Identifying Opposites: Verbs

Match each verb with its opposite.

1. _____ trace   a. forbid   5. _____ lack   e. end
2. _____ heed   b. have   6. _____ trigger   f. accept
3. _____ tolerate   c. lose   7. _____ banish   g. ignore
4. _____ unveil   d. alleviate   8. _____ aggravate h. hide

Chicago Tribune

Postreading

III. Working with Idioms and Expressions

Study the meanings of the idioms and expressions below. A form of each one appears in the paragraph indicated in parentheses.

finish up (1) complete, finish

make someone sick (5) cause to be ill; make very uncomfortable

clear up (6) become less bad

be an education (8) teach a person something

be a market for (8) be wanted by consumers

cope with (13) deal with

peel away (15) pull off

learning curve (16) the time and effort needed to do a job the first time

have plenty of company (17) many others agree or are in the same situation

bottom line (18) final proof; most important truth about something

Answer the following questions:

1. If someone likes action movies, does he *have plenty of company*?
2. If someone has a difficult job, does she need to *cope with it* or *peel it away*?
3. Can you think of any tasks that have a high *learning curve*?
4. If someone says, "Buying my first car *was a real education* for me," what does he mean?
5. When will you *finish up* your college education?

IV. Analyzing Paragraphs

Understanding Transitional Words and Phrases

In the first sentence of a new paragraph, a writer often refers to information that was in the previous paragraph, either by repeating an important word or by using a pronoun to substitute for it. For example, paragraph 3 of the article begins with the pronoun *that,* referring to the examples given in paragraphs 1 and 2. The first sentence of each paragraph listed below contains a noun or pronoun that refers to a key word in the preceding paragraph. On a separate sheet of paper, write the transition words for the following paragraphs: 4, 5, 6, 8, 15, and 18.

V. Talking and Writing

Discuss the topics below. Then choose one of them to write about.

1. Would you be interested in buying a house such as this one? Why or why not?
2. In your native country, is the idea that one's house may be a source of environmental danger a common concern?
3. The topic of health is extremely common in the United States. People read about health issues in newspapers and magazines and watch reports about health and medicine on television news. Is health a common topic of discussion in your native country? Why do you think people discuss it so much in the United States?

Chicago Tribune

Focus on Culture

Setting the Scene

In the United States people love their homes. They love to think about, talk about, decorate, rearrange, maintain, and reconstruct their homes, whether "home" is an apartment, a condominium, or a house with a yard. They therefore find the process of looking for, buying, and selling a home an intensely interesting subject of discussion, and they feel a strong need for solid information about all their concerns.

Newspapers fulfill this need. The *Chicago Tribune,* for example, has three separate sections appearing at various times of the week devoted exclusively to homes. "Your Place" is a weekly guide to apartment living and home buying and selling. It contains real estate advertising and a guide to apartments for rent. "New Homes" contains articles about what to look for in a new house, trends in housing construction and design, and advertising for various new housing. "Home" is about physical aspects of a home, inside and outside: furniture, trends in decorating, home improvement tips, gardening, landscaping.

Articles about homes can also be found in other areas of the newspaper: business news, community news, and lifestyle feature stories frequently are about home matters.

Here are some common topics of newspaper stories about homes:

furniture	mortgage rates	garden plants
choosing a location	indoor plants	apartment market
appliances	home design	tools
luxury homes	decks	new home building trends
barbecuing	renters' rights	shopping
house cleaning	home repairs	legal problems
buying a house	yards	buying a condo
selling a house	heating and air conditioning	carpentry
contractors	home security	kitchens

Articles about homes can have different sorts of purposes. Some of them are *how-to* articles instructing readers about the steps involved in buying, selling, maintaining, improving, and decorating a house. Others are *informative* feature articles about general developments in home-related matters. Others are question-answer *advice* columns about problems in owning a home or renting an apartment. Still others are *essays* detailing personal experiences with situations in the home.

Chicago Tribune

Focus on Culture

Exercise 1. Finding Articles About Homes

Over a two-week period scan your local newspaper for stories about home topics. Fill in the chart below with the following information: (1) the headline of the article, (2) the topic of the article (use the list on page 144 or add your own), (3) the purpose—how-to, informative, advice, essay, and (4) whether or not the article was helpful or interesting to you in some way (yes or no).

	Headline	Topic	Purpose	Helpful or Interesting?
1.				
2.				
3.				
4.				
5.				
6.				

Exercise 2. Analyzing an Article About Homes

Choose the most interesting and helpful article from those listed above and answer these questions about it.

1. What is the main idea of the article?
2. Does the writer communicate this idea clearly? How could the article be better?
3. Is the article accompanied by a photograph or illustration? Describe it.
4. Does the writer quote any experts on the topic? Who are they?
5. Look up three words whose meanings are not clear to you in the dictionary and write their definitions.
6. Why is this article interesting or helpful to you?
7. Would such an article appear in a newspaper in your native country? Explain.
8. Which information in this article would appear in a newspaper in your native country? Which information would appear in a newspaper in your native country that you don't find in this article? Explain.

Chicago Tribune

Focus on Culture

Exercise 3. Finding a Dream House

For anyone who has any interest in buying a home or renting an apartment, the real estate advertising section is extremely valuable. This section contains ads, many of them accompanied by photographs, of houses for sale. When people begin looking for a house or apartment, they look over these ads to get a quick general idea of prices and neighborhoods. Much can be discovered about a city this way. Is a big new house inexpensive? Probably the location is not considered very valuable. Is the rent for a small studio apartment expensive? The location must be very much in demand.

Look through the real estate ads in your local newspaper. Find a house for sale that looks very attractive to you. Then answer the following questions about the ad:

1. Is a style of architecture mentioned, such as ranch, Tudor, Georgian, or colonial? Look up the term in a dictionary if you are not sure of its meaning.
2. What is the location of the house?
3. Is the house newly constructed?
4 What is the price?
5. How many bedrooms and bathrooms are there?
6. Is it a frame or a brick house?
7. Are any special features mentioned, such as a fireplace or new plumbing?
8. What do you like about the house?

Exercise 4. Understanding Apartment Ads

In most real estate sections of newspapers, apartment ads are very brief and use many abbreviations. Here are a few of them:

AC air conditioning	**util** utilities (such as heat and electricity)
BR bedroom	**hdwd flrs** hardwood floors
BA bath	**prkg** parking
pvt private	**w/fp** with fireplace

Next, find a short ad for an apartment. Write out the ad using complete sentences and no abbreviations.

For example: "sunny 1BR hdwd flrs, attract build, $600/mo"

Written out in complete sentences, this ad would read "The apartment is sunny and has one bedroom and hardwood floors. It is in an attractive building, and the rent is $600 per month."

Exercise 5. Journal Assignment: Ask for Answers

Many newspapers publish question-answer columns about common house and apartment problems faced by readers. Write a short letter each day for five days asking about a separate problem related to your home. Here are a few possible topics: furniture, painting, cleaning, garden, grass, appliances, pets, closets, plumbing, roof, neighbors, and noise.

Chicago Tribune

SectionNine

The Nation and the World

Focus on Culture

The Nation and the World

Chicago Tribune

The Nation and the World

Ideals, Values, and Group Identity

"The land of the free and the home of the brave." These closing words of the U.S. national anthem, "The Star Spangled Banner," sum up the ideals that many citizens of the United States have for their country. Ideals and values play an important role in the cultural life of the United States, just as they do in any country.

One of the most important ideals of the United States—and an important part of the way many people in the United States see themselves—is that of freedom. From the time of the American Revolution, when the colonists declared independence from England, the United States has attracted people seeking freedom.

A second ideal of great importance in the United States is that of rule by the people. The framers of the Constitution of the United States strove to ensure that political power would lie in the hands of the voters, not a king or dictator. So they created a *federal* government composed of three branches—legislative, executive, and judicial—to prevent any one part of the government from becoming too powerful. The balance of power among these branches is called the system of *checks and balances*. Also, by reserving much political power for the states that form the national union, the framers strove to prevent the federal government itself from becoming too powerful. This system was hailed by President Abraham Lincoln (1861–1865) as "government of the people, by the people, and for the people."

Another key value in the United States is that of the rights of the individual. The Bill of Rights—the first ten *amendments*, or additions, to the Constitution—is intended to safeguard the rights of the individual and guarantee protection from unjust treatment by the government or the majority. The importance of this protection is reflected in newspaper articles about violations of individual rights. Family, minority group, worker, student, and professional issues often revolve around questions of individual rights.

Nonetheless, individuals and groups together contend for prominence in the United States of today. For all of the importance of individualism, group identity also plays an important role in people's cultural values. And many diverse groups, including noncitizens and naturalized immigrants, have an impact on the cultural life of the United States. In the last section of this book, you will read stories that show how a number of differing cultural values come into play.

Chicago Tribune

Preparation

Visiting German students get in tune with America

Previewing the Article

Few experiences can match the thrill of seeing a new country for the first time. But as this article reports, even that experience can't match the kind of rare, intimate look at a country's culture that fifty German high school students had.

The students—all studying music in a small town in Germany—were part of a cultural exchange. In such a program, students from two different countries "exchange" places, each living for a time like a native student in the other country. These programs can be, like this one, for just a brief trip, or they can be for an entire academic year. Probably the most memorable and valuable aspect of such an exchange is living for a time with a family. As these students discovered by eating, sleeping, traveling, playing, and studying with people from the United States, they were able to carry away with them cultural knowledge they could never get in a class.

The article notes that the students were surprised not only by the *differences* between the cultures of Germany and the United States, but also by what they shared: their love of music. The article also has a lesson for people who have grown up in the United States: one of the best ways to see one's own culture is through the eyes of others.

The following terms may help your understanding of the article:

- *Oklahoma, My Fair Lady,* and *Showboat* are American musicals. All have been very successful both as stage plays and films, and all have famous, easily-recognized songs.
- **Galena** is an old, picturesque Illinois town on the Mississippi River.
- **Great America** is a popular large amusement park north of Chicago.

Before You Read

Discuss the following questions:

1. Read the headline. What are the two meanings of *in tune*? What does it mean to *get in tune* with a foreign culture?
2. Have you ever been part of a student exchange and lived with a foreign family in another country? If so, tell about your experience.

As You Read

As you read the article, think about this question: How many of the students' reactions to Chicago come from being German, and how many come from being from a small town?

Visiting German students
get in tune
with
America

By Kelly Womer

1   Michaela Nothelfer thinks Americans drive too much, eat too much fast food and don't recycle enough. Things move at a faster pace in Chicago than in her hometown of Donzdorf, Germany, where farms and mountains fill the skyline instead of glass buildings. "It's another way of life," said Nothelfer, 16.

2   But when it comes to music, there's not much difference. Mozart and Beethoven as well as tunes from "Oklahoma" and "My Fair Lady" sound the same in any language.

3   Nothelfer and 49 other German high school students just wrapped up a 10-day trip to share their musical talents while experiencing life in America.

4   Their destination: Wheeling High School, where they stayed with students' families and performed several concerts.

5   "Some of the students have said this is like a dream," said Ulrich Schafer, conductor of the German choir. "This is a very special event that has changed some of them. It's a wonderful experience."

6   For the German students, it was a whirlwind trip around Chicago. They stopped at the Sears Tower to view the city from above and

Choir members from Rechberg Gymnasium, a high school in Donzdorf, Germany, practice their repertoire at Wheeling High School, where they have been visiting and performing as part of a cultural exchange. Tribune photo by Michael Budrys.

then walked the downtown streets to see museums and stores.

7   They saw "Showboat," went on all the rides at Great America and spent a day in Galena. They also cheered in the stands during their first American high school football game. On their last day here, they sang several concerts for Wheeling students.

8   "It has all been a great time with the families," said Katja Widmann, 19. "Chicago is much bigger than what we're used to." Donzdorf, a small village located about an hour's drive east of Stuttgart, only boasts 11,000 residents.

9   The experience was also an eye-opener for the Wheeling teenagers. Jennifer Roscoe, 15, hosted German student Simone Grupp. "We learned a lot about

Germany and how different things are there," said Roscoe, a freshman orchestra student who plays violin.

10   The German students, who attend Rechberg Gymnasium, also found out that choir, orchestra and band are part of a student's regular class schedule in Wheeling. At their German high school, choir is an extracurricular activity with practices only lasting an hour each week. "Our group got together more on the trip," Grupp said. "I liked the contact and being with new people and in new surroundings."

11   "It shows that music is the universal language and it's a celebration of friendship," said Pat Baudendiste, Wheeling High School principal. "The world is a global village, and we're really not all that far apart after all."

Postreading

I. Getting the Message

After reading the article, choose the best answer for each item.

1. The German students were in Chicago
   a. as part of a nationwide tour.
   b. to experience the American way of life for a short time.
   c. to listen to rock music from the United States.
2. One reason Chicago seemed so different from Germany is that
   a. the students were from a small rural city in Germany.
   b. the students weren't able to see very much of Chicago.
   c. the students felt unwelcome.
3. The German students
   a. liked their stay in the Chicago area.
   b. disliked their stay in the Chicago area.
   c. had no special reaction to their stay in the Chicago area.
4. The German students found that music
   a. was a source of disagreement with the students from the United States.
   b. was something that they enjoyed with the students from the United States.
   c. was not appreciated by the students from the United States.
5. The German students were surprised to learn that
   a. music was part of the normal class schedule at Wheeling High School.
   b. U.S. high schools have sports teams.
   c. people appreciate German music in the United States.

Check your answers with the key on page 165. If you have made mistakes, reread the article to gain a better understanding of it.

II. Expanding Your Vocabulary

Find each word in the paragraph indicated in parentheses. Use context clues to determine the meaning of the word. Choose the best definition.

1. recycle (1)   a. dispose for reuse   b. relocate
2. pace (1)   a. walking   b. speed
3. skyline (1)   a. outline of a city's   b. the horizon
                       tall buildings
4. destination (4) a. fate   b. end of a journey
5. downtown (6)   a. the lower part of a city b. the business section of a city
6. stands (7)   a. act of standing   b. seats in a stadium
7. universal (11)   a. worldwide   b. native to one country

Postreading

III. Working with Idioms and Expressions

Study the meanings of the idioms and expressions below. A form of each one appears in the paragraph indicated in parentheses.

way of life (1) culture, habits, beliefs of a group of people

as well as (2) in addition to

wrapped up (3) ended

whirlwind trip (6) brief, active tour of an area

a great time (8) a pleasurable experience

eye-opener (9) revealing surprise

extracurricular activity (10) organized activity outside the normal schedule of classes at a school

global village (11) the idea that the world is like a small village because of communication and common interests

after all (11) in spite of everything

Answer the questions below. For help, reread the paragraphs indicated in parentheses.

1. Why did the student say that Americans have "another *way of life*" (1)?
2. What aspects of the German students' stay seemed like a *whirlwind trip* (6)?
3. Why was the trip an *eye-opener* for Simone Grupp (9)?
4. What is described as an *extracurricular activity* for the German students (10)?
5. What evidence does the principal of Wheeling High School give that the world seems like a *global village* (11)?

IV. Talking and Writing

Discuss the topics below. Then choose one of them to write about.

1. Reread the first paragraph of the article in which one of the students gives general impressions of the way people live in the United States. In a few sentences write your own general impressions of people in the United States and their way of life.
2. If these students were to stay two years instead of just ten days, how do you think their impressions of the United States would change? Can you get a good understanding of a foreign city on a "whirlwind trip"?
3. In the last paragraph the high school principal calls music the "universal language." Do you agree or disagree with this statement? Can you think of personal experiences with music that affirm or contradict this idea?

Chicago Tribune

Preparation

Lombard adopts English as its official language
Offensive resolution

Previewing the Articles

Should English be the "official language" of Lombard, Illinois? The question raised by the first article here might seem a strange one to ask about a small suburb outside Chicago with very few people who do not speak English. How could such a question even arise?

The question comes up because the English Only movement is a hot political topic in the United States. On one side are those who insist that Congress should declare English the official language of government. They say that all U.S. citizens and residents should learn English, and they believe that a common language is necessary for a common culture. They see the United States as a *melting pot:* a place with different languages and cultures boiled down and mixed into one culture for the country. On the other side of the question are those who say that the English Only movement has arisen because of fear and suspicion of immigrants. Those in this group see the United States as multi-ethnic and multicultural, with a rich variety of languages as a necessary part of its diverse nature. They also point out that the dominance of English in the United States is in no danger.

As the first article here reports, the members of the Village Board of Lombard felt so strongly about the issue that they passed a resolution saying that they favored English as the official language of the village and the country. The second article here is a letter to the editor of the *Chicago Tribune* from someone who argues strongly against Lombard's resolution.

Together, the two articles show how emotional the issue of language and culture can become and to what extent many people associate language with their very cultural identity.

Before You Read

Discuss the following questions:

1. Do you come from—or do you know about—a country where two or more languages are regularly spoken by large numbers of people? Do any problems result? Explain.
2. In many parts of the world, people grow up speaking two or more languages. Most U.S. citizens, however, speak only English. Is this monolingualism a good thing? What are the negative consequences of monolingualism?
3. Have you ever written a letter to the editor of a newspaper? If you did now, what topic would you write about?

As You Read

1. The Village Board of Lombard argues that everyone in the United States should speak English. As you read the first article, look for another reason for the Board's resolution—a practical reason that has nothing to do with the arguments the Board makes.
2. As you read the article and the accompanying letter, think about the differences of viewpoints expressed. Take a side on the issue and try to find persuasive points in the articles for your position.
3. As you read the articles, think about what you would say if you were going to write a letter to the editor on this subject.

Lombard adopts
English as its
official
language

By Lynn Van Matre
TRIBUNE STAFF WRITER

1   As federal lawmakers continue to debate whether to declare English the official language, Lombard has decided the issue on a municipal level.

2   The Village Board recently passed a resolution that declared English the "official language of government in the Village of Lombard" and urged federal legislators to establish English as the country's official language of government.

3   "We believe that a strong contributing factor in our remaining 'united' is our united use of one language," according to the resolution.

4   While such declarations are not unprecedented at the local level—Addison adopted a similar resolution in 1986—spokespersons for the national organization U.S. English and several state and regional municipal groups described the village's move as highly unusual.

5   Roger Huebner, director of legislative programs for the Illinois Municipal League, said he was unaware of similar actions on the part of other local governments in Illinois.

Total Lombard Population Compared with Population of Recent Immigrant Groups and Residents with Low English Skills

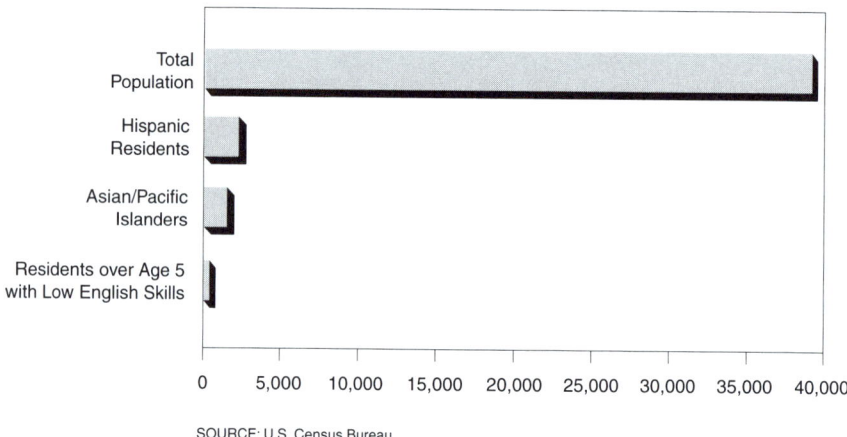

SOURCE: U.S. Census Bureau

6   "Most of the efforts at this point to have English declared the official language are taking place on the federal and state level," said U.S. English spokeswoman Mindy Hess.

7   According to U.S. English statistics, 22 states, including Illinois, have passed legislation designating English the official language, with most of the legislative action taking place since 1980. Three states officially declared English their official language in 1995.

8   The Illinois statute, stating simply that "the official language of the State of Illinois is English," was adopted in 1969.

9   Lombard Village Clerk Lorraine Gerhardt, who drafted the resolution, said she decided to bring the issue to the attention of village trustees after several members of the village staff suggested printing village informational brochures in Spanish this year.

10   "Some of the staff thought it would be a nice thing to do, but

the board was very upset by that idea," Gerhardt said. "The extra printing costs would add to the village's expenses, and also the trustees felt that we should let the public know that the village supports the cause of English as our official language. So they asked me to draft a resolution declaring English the official language of government in the village."

11   According to 1990 census, Asians or Pacific Islanders are Lombard's largest minority group, comprising 4.4 percent of the village's 39,408 people. Slightly under 3 percent of the population is of Hispanic origin.

12   Between 7 and 10 percent of students attending Lombard elementary schools speak a combined total of 27 different languages at home, according to Assistant Supt. John Meyer. The most common non-English languages spoken in the home are Indian dialects, Meyer said.

13   The resolution notes: "We in Lombard urge preservation of ethnic customs and family use of foreign languages, thus enriching our society."

14   It also includes the provision that "nothing in this resolution is intended to restrict or violate the application of federal laws mandating the use of multilingual information in certain cases, or to restrict the use of languages other than English by village employees in the conduct of village business where such use is convenient."

15   The resolution also includes a reference to how "devastating separatist actions based on language have dangerously divided our neighbors to the north," referring to the Canadian separatist controversy in Quebec.

16   However, some Hispanic groups see the village resolution as similarly divisive.

17   "The resolution is moronic and idiotic," said Edward Pelayo, legal department coordinator for Consilio Hispano/Hispanic Council, a Bensenville-based advocacy group with more than 100,000 members in Chicago and suburbs, including Lombard.

18   "I would say that it will divide people, and it puts Hispanics in a bad spot because a lot of Hispanics don't speak English,"

Pelayo added. "There is a lot of anti-Latino sentiment now with things like Proposition 187 in California (which would deny undocumented immigrants the right to social and educational services). Resolutions like this don't help."

19   Village manager Bill Lichter said that so far he has heard no complaints about the resolution from anybody in Lombard.

20   "The intent of the resolution was not to be divisive in any manner," Lichter said.

21   "In the long run, I think the resolution can help prevent divisiveness," Gerhardt said. "It's not anti-anybody."

Voice of the People

Offensive resolution

1   Your Dec. 18 story headlined "Lombard adopts English as its official language" (MetroDuPage) reports that after its staff suggested that village brochures appear in English and Spanish, the village Board of Lombard passed a resolution declaring English the official language of its government.

2   The article quotes statistics on the ethnicity of the residents of Lombard, a community of 39,408. Ethnicity, of course, says nothing about ability to speak English. According to the 1990 census, only 359 residents of Lombard over age 5 cannot speak English well. So what is the Village Board trying to do?

3   Village Manager Bill Lichter says, "The intent of the resolution was not to be divisive in any manner." But the fact is the board sacrificed the sense of belonging and community in the village by grandstanding about the very divisive national struggle over English-only legislation. And by urging Congress and the president to pass such legislation, the Village Board plays on the unfounded fear that immigration threatens the predominance of English in the United States. The facts speak otherwise. Most studies show that immigrants today are learning English faster than immigrants in previous generations.

4   We strongly urge the Village of Lombard to content itself with the management of its proper jurisdiction. The residents of Lombard, especially those whom the board alienated while overstepping its jurisdiction, deserve nothing less than their undivided commitment.

David Marzahl, Waheed Hussain
Illinois Coalition for Immigrant and Refugee Protection

Chicago Tribune

Postreading

I. Getting the Message

After reading "Lombard adopts English as its official language" and "Offensive resolution," choose the best answer for each item.

1. The village resolution applies
   a. to all language use in the village.
   b. only to conversations by village employees.
   c. only to official government publications.

2. The immediate reason why the resolution was passed was
   a. a request to print brochures in Spanish.
   b. a request to create a multilingual elementary school.
   c. a request to create a special language program in a high school.

3. One purpose of the resolution is to
   a. prevent existing federal laws from being enforced in Lombard.
   b. announce that Lombard supports the cause of English as the nation's official language.
   c. force schools to teach only English.

4. At least one opponent of the resolution maintains that it is
   a. anti-Asian.
   b. anti-Hispanic.
   c. too hard to enforce.

5. What percentage of students in Lombard elementary schools speak English at home?
   a. about 90 percent
   b. about 7 percent
   c. about 30 percent

6. How many Lombard residents over age five speak English well?
   a. all of them
   b. about 360
   c. about 39,000

Check your answers with the key on page 165. If you have made mistakes, reread the article to gain a better understanding of it.

II. Expanding Your Vocabulary

A. Getting Meaning from Context

Find each word in the paragraph indicated in parentheses. Use context clues to determine the meaning of the word. Choose the best definition.

Article 2A

1. adopts (headline)	a. agrees	b. approves
2. designating (7)	a. specifying, naming	b. criticizing
3. dialects (12)	a. varieties of one language	b. different languages
4. mandating (14)	a. ordering	b. asking
5. devastating (15)	a. unimportant	b. disastrous

Article 2B

1. unfounded (3)	a. unreasonable	b. uninteresting
2. predominance (3)	a. structure	b. authority
3. alienated (4)	a. offended	b. helped

Chicago Tribune

Postreading

B. Studying Vocabulary About Government

Find each term from the left column in the paragraph indicated in either article A or B.
Reread the paragraph. Match each occupation with a definition in the right column.

1. _____ municipal (A, paragraph 1)
2. _____ federal level (A, paragraph 6)
3. _____ legislation (A, paragraph 7)
4. _____ board (A, paragraph 2)
5. _____ Congress (B, paragraph 3)
6. _____ jurisdiction (B, paragraph 4)

a. the national government
b. territory of a government
c. the U.S. House and Senate
e. laws
f. local
g. governing body of a town, village, or county

III. Working with Idioms and Expressions

Study the meanings of these idioms and expressions. A form of each appears in the indicated paragraph of the article.

Article 2A

pass legislation (7) make a bill a law
bring to someone's attention (9) alert or show someone
put in a bad spot (18) place in an unfavorable situation
in the long run (21) eventually, in the end

Article 2B

say nothing about (2) not reveal anything
grandstanding (3) attempting to impress others by speaking about important matters
deserve nothing less (4) deserve a minimum of something

Answer the following questions:

1. Has the U.S. government *passed legislation* making English the official language?
2. Why does one critic of the resolution say that it *puts* Hispanics in a *bad spot?*
3. *In the long run,* what do you think will be the effect of resolutions to make English the official language of the United States?
4. Why would the ethnicity of a person *say nothing about* that person's ability to speak English?

IV. Talking and Writing

Discuss the topics below. Then choose one of them to write about.

1. Do you agree with the Village Board of Lombard or with the writer of the letter to the editor? Explain.
2. Have you ever experienced discrimination because the language you speak is not the dominant language of a country? Have you ever felt that people made assumptions about you simply on the basis of your language? Discuss your experience.
3. Do you speak two or more languages fluently? How has this ability affected your life and attitudes? Would you recommend that all people study other languages?

Chicago Tribune

Preparation

Political progress reported

Previewing the Article

"If there is one message that echoes forth from this conference, let it be that human rights are women's rights and women's rights are human rights, once and for all."

These inspiring words of Hillary Rodham Clinton at the September, 1995, United Nations 4th World Conference on Women in Beijing, China, were applauded around the world by people eager to see the situation of women improve. The purpose of this conference was to write a platform of proposals regarding the rights of women and to put pressure on all the governments of the world to recognize that women must have the same human rights that are accorded to the men in their countries.

The issue arises all over the globe. For example, there are countries where women cannot own property and where brides can be killed for having dowries that are considered too small by their husbands. Some governments forbid women access to higher education and others, such as many "developed" Western societies, where women still struggle for equal salaries with men.

This article summarizes a report that follows up the Beijing conference. Bella Abzug, the colorful ex-congressperson from New York and the head of the organization that sponsored the report, finds that the Women's Conference was a successful start to a long worldwide campaign.

Before You Read

Discuss the following questions:
1. In your native country do you think that women are treated fairly? Do they have the same legal rights as men?
2. Are you or do you know a woman who has experienced discrimination in some way? Explain.
3. Discuss the meaning of these terms: *feminism, women's groups, gender-neutral language, Ms., politically correct, sexism.*

As You Read

As you read, look for the answers to the following questions:
1. Do the authors of the report think that the United States has moved forward with women's rights in the year after the conference?
2. What does Bella Abzug say about Muslim women's groups? Why is this significant?

Political progress reported

By Mark Wukas
SPECIAL TO THE TRIBUNE

1   Women around the world have sustained the impetus from 1995's UN 4th World Conference on Women in Beijing by increasing their political participation and establishing progressive women's movements in their countries, says a report by the Women's Environment and Development Organization.

2   "I think there's a tremendous amount of activity on the part of women and government that never had been evident before," says Bella Abzug, president and co-founder of the organization, which is based in New York.

3   "The conference created tremendous enthusiasm, passion and determination in women to make sure that their governments don't make this another document to put on the shelf."

4   The organization's report, "Beyond Promises: Governments in Motion One Year after the Beijing Women's Conference," contains 53 reports from 51 countries and territories and two regional reports for countries in the Caribbean and Pacific Islands.

5   Among its questions, the survey asked each country participating in Beijing what, if any, efforts were made to report on the conference results to its women, what institution had it designated to review and implement the conference Platform for Action, what specific initiatives it had undertaken and what resources it had made available to implement the platform.

6   The report allows governments some leeway by referring to them as "in motion" toward implementing reforms, but "30,000 women make a big difference, and 180 governments feel on the spot," says Abzug.

7   For example, the report notes that the United States approved the $1.6 billion Violence Against Women Act, supported working women, increased the minimum wage and expanded health insurance coverage. On the other hand, it cites the United States for rolling back welfare.

8   The report says that most governments reported setting up institutional mechanisms or drafting plans to follow up on commitments they made at Beijing, and that non-governmental activists are playing a role in these follow-up mechanisms. However, some democracies, such as Austria, Canada and New Zealand, have been slow to implement these measures.

9   The 53 respondents to the questionnaire is well below the 189 UN member states that attended the Beijing conference.

10   "Some governments have not reported, and they're dragging their feet," says Abzug. "We haven't had as much response from governments in the Middle East. Those nations have been repressive as far as women are concerned.

11   "Nevertheless, the emergence of Muslim women's groups in the last year has been enormous," she says. "They're being created with a passion, a boldness that I have not seen. Even the women in Islamic nations have been galvanized into creating groups."

12   Abzug says women are through listening to promises and now are demanding action.

13   "We've had a lot of words on equality, now we want the music, which is the action," she says. "As we move into the 21st Century, you'll see much greater participation of women in public and private sectors and more demands for economic justice."

Chicago Tribune

Postreading

I. Getting the Message

After reading the article, indicate if each item is true (T) or false (F).

1. _____ The source of information for this article is a report by the United States State Department.
2. _____ According to Bella Abzug, the 1995 UN 4th World Conference on Women in Beijing has helped women's movements all over the world.
3. _____ The report contains replies from nearly all the countries that attended the Beijing conference.
4. _____ The main purpose of the report was to see what specific action each government had taken to create reforms during the previous year.
5. _____ The report criticized the United States for reducing welfare benefits.
6. _____ Bella Abzug believes that governments in Islamic nations do not respond favorably to issues of women's rights.
7. _____ Bella Abzug is hopeful about Muslim women in Islamic nations because they are creating more women's groups despite the repressive attitudes of their governments.

Check your answers with the key on page 165. If you have made mistakes, reread the article to gain a better understanding of it.

II. Expanding Your Vocabulary

Find each word in the paragraph indicated in parentheses. Then choose the best definition.

1. sustained (1)   a. strengthened   b. strained
2. impetus (1)   a. weakness   b. moving force
3. progressive (1)   a. aiding established   b. aiding reform
                         conditions
4. tremendous (2)   a. frightening   b. a large amount
5. designated (5)   a. chosen   b. criticized
6. implement (5)   a. put into action   b. hold a meeting
7. initiatives (5)   a. first actions   b. completed tasks
8. cites (7)   a. quotes   b. criticizes
9. emergence (11)   a. suppressing, keeping down b. coming out

III. Working with Idioms and Expressions

Study the meanings of the following idioms and expressions:

on the part of (2) by someone or something
put on the shelf (3) disregard
allow some leeway (6) permit freedom of action so someone can succeed
on the spot (6) in a difficult situation
drag their feet (10) intentionally delay acting
to be through (12) to be finished; to stop tolerating

Chicago Tribune

Postreading

Answer the following questions:

1. In paragraph 6 why does referring to governments as "in motion" on reforms *allow* these governments *leeway*?
2. In paragraph 6 why do governments feel *on the spot*?
3. In paragraph 10 how does Bella Abzug know that some governments are *dragging their feet*?
4. In paragraph 12 what are women *through* doing?

IV. Making Sense of Sentences

Parallelism in sentence structure means that whenever a sentence contains two or more parts, those parts should be similar in structure. For example, the long sentence in paragraph 5 would be confusing if the clauses were not parallel in form.

> Among its questions, the survey asked each country participating in Beijing *what, if any, efforts were made* to report on the conference results to its women, *what institution had it designated* to review and implement the conference Platform for Action, *what specific initiatives it had undertaken* and *what resources it had made* available to implement the platform.

The four clauses beginning with *what + noun + a past or past perfect verb* make the sentence clear. All these clauses are objects of the main verb *asked*.

Rewrite the following sentence using parallel structure. Begin the sentence this way: *Bella Abzug believes that . . .*

> Bella Abzug believes in women's right to equal treatment under the law for women, that all women have a right to good health care, and she thinks women should have more jobs.

V. Talking and Writing

Discuss the following topics. Then choose one of them to write about.

1. Bella Abzug spoke particularly about Muslim women. What do you know about the Muslim faith and its attitude toward women's role? Do any other religions have similar beliefs?
2. The quotation from Hillary Clinton in the "Previewing the Article" section expresses a basic moral principle of the women's movement, that women are equal to men. But people in some cultures may not agree with this principle. Is it right for the women's conference to try to impose its idea on cultures that have a different idea of the role of women?
3. In many countries, more and more mothers have jobs outside the home. From the point of view of the women's movement, this is a positive development. Some people, however, see this fact as adversely affecting families and children. What do you think?

Chicago Tribune
Focus on Culture

Setting the Scene

Reading the daily newspaper is a marvelous way to see how people in the United States view themselves and their role in the world at large. On the one hand, a foreign reader of U.S. newspapers might note how critical people in the United States are of themselves. Much of the news is about people behaving badly in one way or another: crimes, fires, scandals, political blunders, economic misfortune, all caused by people and the institutions that they have created for themselves. But the norm in U.S. society is to speak about these problems openly.

On the other hand, the free expression that the newspaper itself represents is something people are proud of. The intense criticism of politicians and the close investigation of government by reporters are examples of freedom of speech in action. They are also examples of American optimism, the belief that life can be constantly improved by the right kind of vigorous action. And newspapers help provide information so that people can take action.

Information about how people in the United States view their nation and the world can be found in many places in a newspaper.

- **The News Section** usually contains factual reporting and news analysis of international and national news. There are also news summaries that give short overviews of events. The *Chicago Tribune,* for example, has a column of short news stories called "Around the World" and another called "Across the Nation."

- **The Op-Ed Section** has several regular features: *editorials,* which express the newspaper's official opinion on national and international events; *letters to the editor,* short essays by readers responding to newspaper stories or to the news itself; *guest essays* (or *op-ed pieces*), by writers or experts in certain fields; *columns* by staff newspaper columnists; and *political cartoons* by artists expressing opinion on some well-known story in the news. The *Chicago Tribune* also has a big Sunday section called "Perspective," which contains news analysis and essays of opinion.

- **The Features Section** contains articles about various aspects of national life: lifestyle trends, health-care concerns, and regional issues are a few of the areas that reveal views of the nation and the world.

- **The Book Review Section,** appearing in most newspapers on Sunday, is an excellent source of essays about the international and national scene.

- **Opinion Columns** are extremely popular sources of opinion about national and world politics. These are short essays by staff writers or *syndicated* writers (whose articles appear in many newspapers at the same time).

Chicago Tribune

Focus on Culture

Exercise 1. Finding the Positive and the Negative

The daily newspaper presents a good picture of how people view themselves, and many of the stories reflect either a positive or a negative idea that people have of their society. Sometimes one story reflects both. For example, a news story about a fund-raising event for homeless people may reflect the sad division between rich and poor in the country but might also show the basic generosity of many people toward less fortunate people. Positive features of U.S. society revealed in many articles include the following: good higher education, athletic people, a good job market, fine entertainment, a prosperous economy, a fair legal system, and environmental awareness. Among the negative features one can find mentioned are these: discrimination, racism, a large gap between the rich and the poor, obesity, tasteless television and movies, and a weak job market.

Look through the pages of several newspapers to find articles that indicate some of the positive and negative points revealed about the United States and the culture of the country. Make a chart like the one below and write down the headline, whether the view is negative or positive, whether you think this topic or issue represents an important feature of U.S. culture, and why.

	Headline	Positive or Negative?	Important Feature?	Why?
1.				
2.				
3.				
4.				
5.				

Exercise 2. Understanding a Political Cartoon

Turn to the editorial page of a daily newspaper and find a political cartoon. Then answer the following questions about it.

1. What news story is the cartoon about? Are you familiar with this story?
2. Describe the cartoon. What is happening in it? Are any physical features of famous people exaggerated in the cartoon? What are they?
3. What words does the cartoon contain? Do you understand them? Use a dictionary to look up the ones you do not know.
4. Is the cartoon funny? Why?
5. What is the point of view expressed by the cartoon? Do you agree with it?
6. Would such an opinion be publicly expressed in your native country?

Chicago Tribune

Focus on Culture

Exercise 3. Reading an Op-Ed Essay

On the page opposite the editorials in most newspapers are columns of opinion by staff writers and guest essays called op-ed articles. Find an op-ed essay and answer the following questions:

1. Who is the author? Is the author identified as the writer of a book or as associated with some organization?
2. What is the main point of the article?
3. How does the writer develop the essay? Does the writer use examples, tell a story, compare the situation with some other situation, use statistics, or some combination of all these?
4. Write two terms used in the article that are unfamiliar to you and define them.
5. Do you agree with the essay? Do you think the essay was weak in some respects?

Exercise 4. Journal Assignment: Following an International Story

What is the place of the United States in the world? Newspapers contain many answers to this question every day. For example, the president may propose dealing with a military crisis in a foreign nation with a new economic, political, or military policy. Newspapers then report the president's views objectively in news stories and analyze them in news analysis features by its Washington reporters, staff columnists, and editorial page writers. As long as the controversy seems newsworthy, the discussion of it will appear almost daily in the newspaper.

Scan the front page of your local newspaper for an important international story. Follow this story for a week and answer these questions about it.

1. What is the headline of the *news story*? What are the basic facts of the situation?
2. How many articles appear in the newspaper each day related to this story?
3. Find a *news analysis feature* about the story. These often appear next to the news story. This kind of article gives general background on the situation so that the reader can understand what issues are involved.
4. Find an *editorial* about the story. What does the editorial board of your newspaper think or propose about the issue? Do you agree?
5. Find a *letter to the editor* about the story. What does the writer think? Does the writer agree or disagree with the newspaper? Do you agree with the writer?
6. At the end of the week, find another news story about the topic. What is the headline? How has the situation in the foreign country changed in a week?

Comprehension Check

Answers to "Getting the Message" Exercises

Views of Community
Inside the 'Pilsen/Little Village' exhibit
1. b
2. c
3. a
4. b
5. a
6. a

Do names come naturally?
1. T
2. T
3. F
4. T
5. F
6. F
7. F
8. T
9. T

The World of Business and Work
Cubicle, sweet cubicle
1. T
2. F
3. T
4. F
5. T
6. T
7. T
8. F

Companies that still make people—not profit—top priority
1. F
2. T
3. F
4. F
5. T
6. T
7. T
8. T

Lifestyles
Tales in English give fresh voice to foreign lands
1. a
2. b
3. b
4. a
5. a

The delights of downsizing
1. a
2. a
3. a
4. c
5. b

New Year's wish list runs from fitness to forests
1. F
2. T
3. F
4. F
5. F

Sports
Triumphant return to Titletown

Nothing cheesy about Green Bay
1. a
2. b
3. c
4. b
5. a

How far south does Packerland go?
1. F
2. F
3. T
4. T
5. T
6. T
7. F
8. F

Failure to recognize proved costly
1. a
2. a
3. a
4. a
5. a
6. c
7. c

Food & Restaurants
What! No turkey?
1. F
2. T
3. T
4. F
5. T
6. T
7. T
8. F
9. T

The land of the bland
1. b
2. a
3. a
4. c
5. b
6. a

Leisure Time
Natural selection
1. b
2. b
3. b
4. a
5. a

A party in a basket
1. a
2. b
3. c
4. a
5. c

Religion
Xers finding faith their destination
1. a
2. b
3. b
4. c
5. b
6. a
7. a

Church singles groups find way to loosen up, keep faith
1. a
2. c
3. b
4. a
5. b
6. b
7. b

Religious groups push campaign fund reforms
1. F
2. F
3. F
4. T
5. F
6. T
7. F

At Home
Enough of these holidays! Your body is set to give up
1. a
2. b
3. c
4. a
5. c
6. c
7. c

School's still out, but for parents, it's no vacation
1. b
2. b
3. c
4. a
5. c

Sick of your house? Do we have a home for you!
1. F
2. T
3. T
4. F
5. T
6. T
7. F
8. F

The Nation and the World
Visiting German students get in tune with America
1. b
2. a
3. a
4. b
5. a

Lombard adopts English as its official language

Offensive resolution
1. c
2. a
3. b
4. b
5. a
6. c

Political progress reported
1. F
2. T
3. F
4. T
5. T
6. T
7. T